Success AS Sociology

The Complete Revision Guide

✓ Provides the key knowledge and AO2 skills for exam success

✓ Advice on exam technique from senior examiners

✓ Practice questions for you to try

✓ Examples of top-grade student answers

Designed by expert examiners to boost your grade

The ONLY AS Sociology revision book written by Chief and Principal Examiners

Rob Webb and Keith Trobe

NAPIER PRESS *Sociology*

Published by Napier Press
PO Box 6383
Brentwood
CM13 2NQ
Email: napierpress@aol.com
Website: www.sociology.uk.net

ISBN-10: 0954007972
ISBN-13: 978-0954007973

The authors assert the moral right to be identified as the authors of this work.

British Library Cataloguing in Publication Data
A catalogue record for this book is available from the British Library

Design by HL Studios
Printed and bound by Vertis Group Ltd

NAPIER PRESS *Sociology*

Go to www.sociology.uk.net
On-line support for AS and A level Sociology teachers and students.

Contents

CHAPTER 1 FAMILIES AND HOUSEHOLDS

1 Couples

Key Issues

▶ Are couples becoming more equal?

▶ Does women being in paid work make a difference to the domestic division of labour?

▶ Who takes the decisions and controls the family's resources?

▶ How significant is domestic violence in couple relationships?

Sociologists are interested in whether couples are equal or not. We can look at it in terms of the domestic division of labour, decision making and control of resources, and domestic violence.

The domestic division of labour

The division of labour refers to the roles men and women play, e.g. housework, childcare, paid work. Do they share these equally? There are different views:

Functionalism

Parsons (1955) identifies two conjugal (marital) roles: **the instrumental role** of the male breadwinner and **the expressive role** of the female nurturer/carer.

Parsons argues that this gender division of labour among couples is functional for the family, its members and wider society. He sees this division as biologically based – women are naturally suited to nurturing, men to providing – so everyone benefits from this specialisation.

The New Right agree with Parsons that this biologically based gender division of labour is the best way of organising family life.

The 'march of progress' view

This view sees conjugal roles becoming more equal in modern society. Bott (1957) identifies two types:

▶ **Segregated conjugal roles** are separate. There is a sharp division of labour between male breadwinner and female homemaker (like Parsons' instrumental and expressive roles). Husband and wife spend their leisure separately.

▶ **Joint conjugal roles** involve couples sharing domestic tasks and leisure.

Young and Willmott (1962) found segregated conjugal roles in working-class extended families in Bethnal Green in the 1950s.

▶ **Men** were the breadwinners. They were not involved in the home, spending their leisure with workmates.

▶ **Women** were full-time housewives and childcarers. Female relatives helped each other and spent their leisure together.

Interpretation

Is the question about a particular form of inequality (e.g. domestic labour)? If so, stick to this. Or is it about inequality more generally? If so, cover decision making, resources and domestic violence as well.

Evaluation

Feminists reject the functionalist view – the division of labour is not 'natural' (e.g. it is not found in all societies) and it only benefits men.

The symmetrical family Young and Willmott (1973) see a long-term trend towards joint conjugal roles and the symmetrical family, where roles are more similar and equal:

▶ Most women now go out to work.

▶ Men help with housework and childcare (the 'new man').

▶ Couples spend their leisure time together. Men have become more home-centred and the family more privatised.

Analysis
When discussing the symmetrical family, don't just describe it – explain the reasons why it has arisen.

Reasons The rise of the symmetrical family is due to major social changes during the 20th century, e.g. higher living standards, labour-saving devices, better housing, women working, smaller families.

Feminism

Feminists reject the march of progress view. They see the family as patriarchal (male dominated), *not* symmetrical or equal. Women still do most of the housework and childcare.

The housewife role Oakley (1974) argues that the housewife role is the primary role for women. It is the result of industrialisation and factory production in the 19th century, which led to the separation of paid work from the home.

Application
In questions on domestic labour, don't stop at Willmott and Young vs. Oakley. You must bring in more up-to-date material to get a reasonable mark.

▶ **Women were excluded from the workforce** and confined to the home. Men became the sole breadwinners, resulting in women's economic dependence.

▶ **The housewife role is socially constructed**, not 'natural' (unlike the functionalist and New Right view).

Oakley found no evidence of symmetry in domestic labour. She argues that Young and Willmott exaggerate men's role: although husbands 'helped', this could include just ironing their own shirt once a week.

Boulton (1983) argues that we need to look at who is *responsible* for tasks, not just who performs them. The wife is seen as responsible for children's welfare, even when men 'help'. Less than one in five husbands took a major part in childcare.

The impact of women working

Most women today are in paid work. Some sociologists argue that this is leading to a more equal division of domestic labour.

Evaluation
Crompton argues that change has been due to economic factors, not values. Women's increasing earning power means men have to do more in the home – but men still earn more, so the division of labour is still unequal.

Gershuny: lagged adaptation

Gershuny (1994) found that:

▶ Men whose wives worked full-time did more domestic work (though they still only did 27% of it).

▶ This is a result of a change in values and role models or 'lagged adaptation': couples are gradually adapting to women working full-time.

▶ But domestic tasks are still sex-typed (e.g. men do the DIY).

The commercialisation of housework

Analysis
Point out that not all couples are in the same economic position. Class and income differences play an important part in influencing the domestic division of labour.

Couples cam can now buy in goods and services instead of women having to produce them at home, e.g. ready meals, nurseries etc cut the amount of domestic labour needed. Schor (1993) argues that this has led to the 'death of the housewife role' – but only for the better-off.

The dual burden

Feminists argue that women in paid work has not led to equality, but simply to the dual burden of paid work plus domestic work. Men benefit from this:

▶ **Ferri and Smith** (1996) found that women working has had little impact on the division of labour – under 4% of fathers were the main child-carer.

▶ **Morris** (1990) found that even where the wife was working and the husband unemployed, she still did most of the housework. The men suffered a crisis of masculinity – having lost their breadwinner role, they resisted taking on the feminine domestic role.

The triple shift Duncombe and Marsden (1995) found that women were required not only to carry a dual burden, but a triple shift: emotion work, domestic labour and paid work.

Same-sex couples and gender scripts

Radical feminists argue that heterosexual relationships are inevitably patriarchal and unequal – even when women are in paid work. They contrast this with same-sex relationships. For example, Dunne's (1999) study of 37 lesbian couples with children found a more equal division of labour. Dunne uses the idea of gender scripts:

▶ **Heterosexuals** were socialised into gender scripts that set out different masculine and feminine roles and gender identities.

▶ **Lesbians** did not link household tasks to gender scripts, so they were more open to negotiation and thus more equal.

Analysis
Many students don't define accurately or distinguish clearly between dual burden and triple shift. Make sure you do!

Evaluation
However, Dunne found that where one partner did much more paid work, they also did less domestic work – i.e. paid work was still an important influence on the division of labour.

Resources and decision making

Kempson (1994) found that women in low-income families denied their own needs to make ends meet. But even in households with adequate incomes, resources are often shared unequally, leaving women in poverty.

Unequal shares of resources are often the result of who controls the family's income and who makes the decisions about spending it – usually the man.

Decision making and paid work

One reason men take a greater share of resources and demand a bigger say in decisions is because they earn more. This is supported by Pahl and Vogler (1993). They identify two types of control over family income:

▶ **The allowance system**, where men work and give their non-working wives an allowance from which they budget to meet the family's needs.

▶ **Pooling**, where partners work and have joint responsibility for spending, e.g. a joint bank account.

There has been a big increase in pooling in recent years. However, Vogler (1994) found that men still tended to make the major decisions, reflecting their greater earnings.

Application
In questions on the impact of paid work on couples' roles and relationships, explain how it affects decision making and control of resources (and not just domestic labour).

Professional couples and decision making

Edgell's (1980) study of decision making among professional couples where both partners work full-time also found inequalities. Very important decisions (e.g. about finances or moving house) were taken either by the husband alone or with him having the final say. Important decisions were usually taken jointly. Less important decisions (e.g. food purchases), were usually taken by the wife.

Explanations There are two main explanations for inequalities in decision making:

▶ **Economic** Men have more power in decision making because they earn more. Women are economically dependent, so they have less say.

▶ **Patriarchal socialisation** Some feminists argue that gender role socialisation in patriarchal society instils the idea that men are the decision-makers.

Domestic violence

Domestic violence statistics

Domestic violence is too widespread to be just the behaviour of a few 'disturbed' individuals. The British Crime Survey (BCS) estimated that there are 6.6 million assaults per year. However, assaults are not random – they are mainly by men against women.

According to the BCS, nearly one in four women is assaulted by her partner at some time. However, police statistics under-estimate its extent because of under-reporting and under-recording:

Under-reporting Domestic violence is the violent crime least likely to be reported to police. The BCS estimated that under a third of assaults are reported. Yearnshire (1997) found that on average a woman suffers 35 assaults before reporting abuse.

Under-recording Police are often unwilling to record, investigate or prosecute domestic violence because they are reluctant to become involved in the 'private sphere' of the family. They often take the view that individuals are free to leave if unhappy. In fact, many women cannot leave because they and their children are financially dependent on their partners.

The radical feminist explanation

Radical feminists see domestic violence as the result of patriarchy – male domination. In their view, all societies are patriarchal and the key division is between men and women.

▶ Men oppress women, mainly through the family, where they benefit from women's unpaid domestic labour and sexual services. Domestic violence (or the threat of it) enables men to control women, so it is inevitable in patriarchal society.

▶ Men also dominate the state and this explains why the police and courts fail to take domestic violence seriously.

Dobash and Dobash provide supporting evidence. They found violence was triggered when husbands felt their authority was being challenged. They conclude that marriage legitimates violence by giving power to men.

Domestic violence and inequality

Women are not the only group at risk. Other groups likely to be victims include:

▶ children and young people, the poor and lower classes, and alcohol and illegal drug users.

Lack of resources Wilkinson (1996) argues that these patterns are a result of stress on the family caused by social inequality. Families that lack resources – e.g. low income, poor housing – suffer more stress and this increases the risk of violence.

Application

In questions on feminist contributions to our understanding of the family, discuss their work on domestic violence as well as on housework.

Evaluation

Radical feminism explains why most violence is by men against women. It doesn't explain violence by women against men, children or lesbian partners. Elliot (1996) argues that not all men benefit from it.

Evaluation

Wilkinson shows how inequality causes higher levels of stress and violence. However, he doesn't explain why women rather than men are the main victims.

ONE TO TRY

Question Examine the factors affecting the division of domestic labour among couples. (24 marks)

Examiner's Advice Domestic labour includes housework, childcare and emotion work, so examine what sociologists say about these. Use concepts such as the symmetrical family, joint versus segregated conjugal roles, dual burden, triple shift and lagged adaptation, but avoid just writing a descriptive account of studies. Instead focus on factors or reasons such as the impact of paid work, social class differences, patriarchy, geographical mobility, biology etc. Give your answer a theoretical framework by using functionalism, the New Right and feminism – e.g. the first two see the division as biologically based and benefiting everyone, whereas feminists see it as socially constructed, patriarchal and benefiting men.

2 Childhood

Key Issues
▶ In what ways is childhood socially constructed?
▶ Why did the modern notion of childhood develop?
▶ Are children better off today than in the past?
▶ What different views are there about the future of childhood?

Childhood as a social construct

Sociologists see childhood not as a 'natural' category, but as socially constructed, i.e. defined and created by society. What is seen as 'childhood' varies:

▶ between societies (cross-cultural differences)

▶ within societies, e.g. between different classes

▶ historically, over time.

Interpretation
In essays, explain the idea of the social construction of childhood near the start and use it as a framework for your answer.

Cross-cultural differences in childhood
Benedict (1934) argues that children in simpler, non-industrial societies are treated differently from their modern western counterparts:

▶ They have more responsibility at home and work.

▶ Less value is placed on obedience to adult authority.

▶ Children's sexual behaviour is often viewed differently.

Also, the behaviour expected of children and that expected of adults are less clearly separated.

Childhood in the West
Unlike in simpler societies, the modern Western notion of childhood has the following features:

▶ Childhood is seen as a special, innocent time of life.

▶ Children are seen as fundamentally different from adults – as physically immature and not competent to run their own lives.

▶ As a result, they need a lengthy, protected period of nurturing and socialisation.

Analysis
Contrast childhood in traditional and modern societies using concepts like status, separateness, competence and responsibility.

▶ Childhood is a distinct life stage – 'child' is a separate status from 'adult'. According to Pilcher (1995), the key feature of the modern idea of childhood is separateness.

▶ According to Cunningham (2007), children are seen as the opposite of adults, with the right to happiness.

These differences illustrate the key sociological idea that childhood is not fixed in the same form in all societies – different cultures construct it differently.

Historical differences in childhood

The position of children also differs over time. The modern Western idea of childhood is a relatively recent invention. According to Ariès (1960), in medieval Europe, the idea of childhood did not exist.

- Children were not seen as having a different 'nature' from adults.
- Work began from an early age.
- Children were 'mini-adults' with the same rights, duties and skills as adults.

According to Shorter (1975), parental attitudes towards children were very different, e.g. high child death rates encouraged indifference and neglect, especially towards infants.

The modern notion of childhood began to emerge from the 13th century:

- Schools began to specialise only in the education of the young.
- The church increasingly saw children as fragile 'creatures of God' needing discipline and protection from worldly evils.
- There was a growing distinction between children's and adults' clothing, setting children apart from adults.

Ariès argues that this resulted in the emergence of the modern 'cult of childhood'. The 20th century was 'the century of the child'.

Why has the position of children changed?

The position of children has changed due to major social changes during the 19th and 20th centuries:

- **Lower infant mortality rates and smaller families** More infants surviving meant that parents had fewer children and made a greater financial and emotional investment in them.
- **Specialist knowledge about children's health**, e.g. theories of child development stressed that children need supervision and protection.
- **Laws banning child labour** from the 1840s onwards changed children from economic assets to economic liabilities, financially dependent on their parents.
- **Compulsory schooling** since 1880 has created a period of dependency on the family and separated children from the adult world of work.
- **Child protection and welfare laws** and agencies emphasised children's vulnerability and made their welfare a central concern.
- **The idea of children's rights**, e.g. the Children Act (1989) sees parents as having 'responsibilities' towards their children rather than 'rights'.
- **Laws about social behaviour**, e.g. minimum ages for a wide range of activities, from sex to smoking, reinforce the attitude that children are different from adults.

Industrialisation was the underlying cause, e.g. modern industry needs an educated workforce, so compulsory education is needed; higher standards of living resulting from industrialisation lead to lower infant mortality rates.

Has the position of children improved?

There are two competing views of whether children's position has improved.

The 'march of progress' view

Ariès, Shorter and others argue that children's position has been steadily improving and today is better than it has ever been. Family and society have become 'child-centred':

- Children are better cared for in terms of their educational, psychological and medical needs.
- Most babies now survive: the infant mortality rate in 1900 was 154; now it is 5.

Application
Avoid lengthy descriptions of Ariès. Instead, explain the significance of his work and give some examples.

Application
By showing how ideas about children, their status and treatment varied over time, Ariès shows that childhood is socially constructed.

Analysis
Use these factors to draw contrasts with medieval times and conclusions about how childhood has been constructed differently over time.

Interpretation
If a question presents the view that children's position has improved, don't just agree – start by identifying the alternative view as well.

▶ Higher living standards and smaller family sizes mean parents can afford to provide for children's needs.

▶ Children are protected from harm and exploitation by laws against child abuse and child labour.

The conflict view

Conflict theorists, e.g. Marxists and feminists, argue that the 'march of progress' view is an over-generalised and idealised image. It ignores inequalities *among children* and *between children and adults.*

Inequalities among children Third World children have different life chances from those in the West. In Western societies, there are:

▶ **Gender differences**, e.g. girls are expected to do more housework.

▶ **Ethnic differences**, e.g. Asian parents are more likely to be strict towards daughters than sons.

▶ **Class inequalities**, e.g. poor children are more likely to die in infancy or do badly at school.

Inequalities between children and adults 'Child liberationists' such as Firestone (1979) argue that extensive care and protection are just new forms of oppression – e.g. being banned from paid work is not a benefit to children but a form of inequality, subjecting them to even greater adult control.

Age patriarchy

Gittins (1998) argues that there is an age patriarchy of adult domination that keeps children subordinate. For example, adults exercise control over children's time (e.g. bedtimes), space (e.g. where they are allowed to go) and bodies (e.g. what they eat and wear). Adults make children economically dependent by preventing them from working, e.g. through child labour laws. Adult control can lead to physical, sexual or emotional abuse – over 30,000 children are on the child protection register.

Resistance Children may resist the restricted status of 'child' by acting older, e.g. smoking, drinking alcohol etc. For Hockey and James (1993), this shows modern childhood is a status most children want to escape.

The future of childhood

Postman (1994) argues that childhood as we know it is disappearing, and that children are becoming more like adults – gaining similar rights and acting in similar ways, e.g. clothing, leisure, even crime.

For Postman, this is the result of television culture replacing print culture:

▶ **In print culture**, children lacked the literacy skills needed to access information, so adults could keep knowledge about sex, money, violence, illness, death and other 'adult' matters secret from them.

▶ **Television culture** makes information available to adults and children alike. The boundary between adulthood and childhood is broken down and adult authority weakened.

However, Opie (1993) believes childhood is not disappearing, e.g. a separate children's culture continues to exist in the form of games, songs, jokes etc. Others argue that Western norms of what childhood should be – a separate life stage, based in the nuclear family and school – are being exported globally. Western 'childhood' is not disappearing, but spreading.

Analysis
Class, gender and ethnic differences affect life chances in all societies, so it's hard to speak of improvements in the position of children in *general.*

Evaluation
This ignores how adults may use their power to benefit children, e.g. passing laws against child abuse. Some adult control is needed to safeguard children's interests.

Application
Where possible, use examples to illustrate key concepts such as age patriarchy.

Evaluation
Postman over-emphasises a single factor, ignoring others, e.g. rising living standards and legal changes.

'Toxic childhood'

Palmer (2006) argues that rapid technological and cultural changes are damaging children's development, e.g. junk food, computer games, intensive marketing to children, testing in education, long hours worked by parents. As a result, children are deprived of a genuine childhood.

▶ UK youth are at or near the top of international league tables for obesity, self-harm, drug and alcohol abuse, violence and teenage pregnancies.

▶ UNICEF (2007) ranked the UK 21st out of 25 for children's well being.

Evaluation
Not all children are equally affected by these trends – those in higher social classes are less affected.

Change or continuity?

Some aspects of childhood suggest it may be disappearing or changing, others that it is continuing. Much depends on what happens to:

▶ The emphasis on children's rights.

▶ The length of time spent in education.

▶ Children's access to means of communication.

▶ Growing similarities between children and adults in leisure activities, dress, diet etc.

▶ Adult concerns about children's behaviour, discipline and exposure to media sex and violence.

Lee (2001) concludes that childhood has not disappeared, but that it has become more complex and contradictory – e.g. children are important as consumers but dependent on parents for their purchasing power.

ONE TO TRY

Question Examine the effects of social change on the position of children.
(24 marks)

Examiner's Advice Start by pointing out that childhood is not a fixed category but rather is socially constructed and changes over time. Then describe the different ways in which the social position of children has changed (e.g. by contrasting the position of children in medieval times with today) and explain the causes of such changes (e.g. legal and demographic factors).

Contrast the 'march of progress' view with the arguments of conflict sociologists, making use of concepts such as age patriarchy. You can evaluate by considering whether the changes you have examined have led to an improvement in the position of children, or by speculating about the future of childhood.

3 Theories of the Family

Key Issues

▶ How do the main sociological perspectives see the role of the family?
▶ What functions does the family perform?
▶ Who benefits from the family – society, the ruling class or men?

Different sociological perspectives have differing views on the nature and role of the family. These reflect their differing ideas about the nature of wider society. The main perspectives on the family are:

▶ **Functionalism**

▶ **The New Right**

▶ **Marxism**

▶ **Feminism**

▶ **Postmodernism**

Application
When tackling a question on a particular theory of the family, keep your main focus on the theory named in the question – but apply the other theories to evaluate it.

The functionalist perspective

Functionalists see society as based on a value consensus – a shared set of norms and values (or culture). This shared culture enables members of society to co-operate harmoniously to meet society's needs and to achieve their common goals.

The organic analogy
Functionalists see society as being like a biological organism (such as the human body):

▶ The body is made up of different parts (cells, organs etc) that function together to meet its needs and maintain it.

▶ Society is a system made up of different but interdependent parts or sub-systems, such as institutions like the education system, the economy, religion, the state etc.

▶ The function of any part is the contribution it makes to maintaining the social system as a whole.

Evaluation
Functionalists assume the family is harmonious and ignore conflict and exploitation, e.g. child abuse and the oppression of women.

The functions of the family For functionalists, the family plays a vital role in maintaining the social system as a whole, as well as meeting the needs of other sub-systems such as the economy. Functionalists take a positive view of the family, seeing it as performing beneficial functions both for wider society and for all its individual members. However, they disagree to some extent about what these functions are:

Murdock: four functions of the family
G.P. Murdock (1949) argues that the nuclear family performs four essential functions for society and for its members:

▶ **Stable satisfaction of the sex drive** with the same marital partner. This prevents the social disruption that would be caused by a sexual 'free-for-all'.

▶ **Reproduction of the next generation**, without which society would cease to exist.

▶ **Socialisation of the young** into society's norms and values enables new members to integrate into society.

> **Satisfaction of members' economic needs** – e.g. providing food and shelter. In pre-industrial societies, the family is a unit of production (working together), but in modern societies it has become a unit of consumption only.

Evaluation
Functionalists ignore family diversity and assume the nuclear family is the universal norm.

Practicality and universality By performing these functions, the nuclear family helps to maintain social stability. For Murdock, the 'sheer practicality' of the nuclear family as a way of meeting these needs explains why it is universal – found in all human societies.

Parsons' 'functional fit' theory

Parsons (1955) argues that the kinds and range of functions that the family performs depend on the type of society in which it is found. This also determines what kind of structure the family will have. Parsons identifies two types of family structure:

> The three-generational extended family, found in pre-industrial society

> The two-generational nuclear family, found in modern industrial society.

The extended family was multi-functional – it was a unit both of production and of consumption, e.g. all members worked the land together, and it often performed welfare, military, religious or other functions.

The nuclear family fits the two key needs of modern industrial society:

Analysis
Explain why modern societies are likely to have high rates of mobility because of the needs of the economy. Contrast this with a traditional agricultural economy.

> **Geographical mobility** Industries constantly spring up and decline in different places. It is easier for the compact two-generational nuclear family to move to where the jobs are.

> **Social mobility** Because status in industrial society is achieved not ascribed, adult sons can now achieve a higher status than their fathers. Breaking away to set up their own nuclear family unit removes the status conflict that would result if they stayed.

Two irreducible functions The nuclear family is now left with only two 'irreducible' or essential functions:

> **Primary socialisation** of the young, equipping the next generation with basic skills and society's values.

> **Stabilisation of adult personalities**, enabling adults to relax and release tensions so that they can return to the workplace and perform their roles efficiently.

Segregated conjugal roles Parsons distinguishes between the male instrumental (breadwinning) role and the female expressive (nurturing) role. He sees the gender division of labour within the family as biologically based. For example, women give birth and this is why they are suited to the expressive role.

The New Right perspective

This is a political rather than a sociological perspective which has had considerable influence on government policies in Britain and elsewhere. It is a conservative view of the family based on the following assumptions:

Evaluation
Gender roles in the family are not 'natural' (biological), but socially constructed, learned through socialisation and vary between cultures.

> **A biologically based division of labour** Like functionalists, the New Right see the division of labour in the family between a male breadwinner and a female homemaker as natural and biologically determined. Similarly, they believe that a nuclear family with segregated conjugal roles is the best place in which to socialise children.

> **Families should be self-reliant** Reliance on state welfare leads to a dependency culture, undermines traditional gender roles and produces family breakdown and lone parent families. Lack of a male role model for boys results in social problems and delinquency.

The Marxist perspective

Marxism is a conflict view of society. It sees modern capitalist society as divided into two classes:

▶ **The capitalist class** (or bourgeoisie), who own the means of production (the factories, land etc).

▶ **The working class** (or proletariat), who own only their labour, which they are forced to sell to the capitalists in return for wages. This enables the capitalist employer to exploit the working class in order to produce profit.

The functions of the family Marxists see all institutions in capitalist society as contributing to the maintenance of exploitation. The family is seen as an oppressive institution that performs several important functions for capitalism:

Passing on wealth Engels (1884) argues that, as private property became more important, men who controlled it needed to ensure they could pass it to their own sons and this led to monogamous marriage. But this also meant the woman becoming the private property of her husband, who controlled her sexuality to ensure he was the father of her children.

Ideological functions Zaretsky (1976) argues that there is a 'cult of private life' – the belief that we can only gain fulfilment from family life – and this distracts attention from exploitation.

Unit of consumption Capitalism needs consumers to buy its products. The family is an important market for consumer goods and therefore enables capitalists to make profits.

Feminist perspectives

Feminism too is a conflict view that sees the family as oppressing women. There are several different types of feminism:

1. **Liberal feminists** argue that gender inequality is gradually being overcome through legal reforms and policy changes (such as equal pay), challenging stereotypes and changing people's attitudes and socialisation. This is a 'march of progress' view – e.g. the 'new man' is becoming more widespread.

2. **Marxist feminists** argue that capitalism is the main cause of women's oppression in the family and this performs several functions for capitalism:

   ▶ **Reproducing the labour force** Women socialise the next generation of workers and service the current one, for free.

   ▶ **Absorbing men's anger** that would otherwise be directed at capitalism. Wives soak up their husbands' frustration that comes from being exploited at work.

   ▶ **A reserve army of cheap labour**. When not needed, women workers return to their domestic role.

   Marxist feminists argue that women's oppression in the family is linked to exploitation of the working class. Therefore the family must be abolished at the same time as capitalism.

3. **Radical feminists** argue that patriarchy (male domination) is the main cause of women's oppression. The family and marriage are key patriarchal institutions.

   ▶ Men benefit from women's unpaid domestic labour and sexual services.

   ▶ Men dominate women through violence or the threat of it.

   For radical feminists, the patriarchal system must be overturned and the family abolished. Some radical feminists believe in 'political lesbianism' and complete separatism from men.

Analysis
Contrast the Marxist conflict view with the functionalist consensus view of the family. Compare their similarities: both are structural views that see the family as shaped by the wider society.

Application
Use your knowledge about changes outside the family (e.g. work, the law, education) to explain why gender roles within the family might be becoming more equal.

Evaluation
Women's oppression did not start with capitalism, so there is no reason to believe it would end with it. Radical feminists argue that women are not only oppressed by capitalism, but also by patriarchy.

Evaluation
Radical feminists ignore the importance of class and ethnic inequality – e.g. white middle-class women may have more power than black working-class men.

Interpretation
In essays on feminism and the family, interpret the question as being about a range of types of feminism. You can also score analysis marks by explaining the similarities and differences between them.

4. **Difference feminism** argues that not all women share the same experiences of oppression – women of different ethnicities, class backgrounds etc may have different experiences of the family. For example, by regarding the family solely as a source of oppression, white feminists neglect black women's experience of racism. Many black feminists view the black family positively as a source of support in a racist society.

Postmodernism and the family

Marxism and functionalism are 'modernist' theories. As such, they have three features in common:

▶ They are structural theories – they see modern society as having a clear-cut, predictable structure.

▶ They see one particular family type – the nuclear family – as 'fitting' this structure and performing important functions for it.

▶ This means that we can generalise about the type of family to be found in modern society.

Application
Use your knowledge of increased family diversity today to illustrate the postmodernist perspective.

Postmodernists disagree. They argue that, from the late 20th century, society began to move into a 'postmodern' phase – a fundamentally new type of society. The new postmodern society has two key features:

Fragmentation of cultures and lifestyles Individuals now have more choice and are freer to construct their identities and lifestyles as they wish. As a result, society is now more a collection of different subcultures (e.g. different youth subcultures, ethnic groups, consumption patterns), rather than the single shared culture described by functionalists.

Rapid change has made life less predictable and orderly. New technology and the media break down existing barriers of time and space, and transform work and leisure patterns.

Evaluation
People are not always free to make choices – e.g. domestic violence and low pay may restrict women's options.

As a result, the family has become less stable, but there is now more choice about intimate relationships and domestic arrangements. For example, individuals can choose to cohabit, get divorced, have children (own or adopted) outside of marriage, come out as gay, live alone etc. The result of this greater choice is greater family diversity. This means it is no longer possible to generalise about family life in the way that modernist sociologists have done.

ONE TO TRY

Read item A and answer the question that follows.

Item A
The functionalist view of the family is based on a consensus view of society. Functionalists see the family as performing vital positive functions both for society as a whole and for all the individual members of the family. For example, Parsons argues that it is responsible for the primary socialisation of the young, equipping them with basic skills, norms and values to allow them to integrate into society.

However, the functionalist view of the family has been criticised by sociologists from other perspectives, who argue that it ignores conflict and oppression in the family and fails to explain the extent of family diversity.

Question Using material from **Item A** and elsewhere, assess the usefulness of the functionalist view of the family. (24 marks)

Examiner's Advice Start with a brief outline of the general functionalist perspective on society (e.g. the organic analogy). Link this to their view of the family as performing functions for society. You should consider a range of issues, e.g. the functions of the family, functional fit theory and the role of the nuclear family, universality of the family, instrumental and expressive roles etc. Make sure you use material from the Item. For example, you can link issues of conflict and oppression to feminism and Marxism, and diversity to postmodernism, and use these perspectives to evaluate functionalism.

4 Demography

Key Issues

▶ What are the main population trends in the UK since 1900?

▶ What are the causes of changes in birth, fertility and death rates, ageing and migration?

▶ What are the social effects of these population changes?

Interpretation
Address all parts of the question – e.g. if it's about causes *and* effects of a population change, make sure you deal with both.

Population growth

Demography is the study of population, including factors affecting its size and growth. Whether a population is growing, declining or stable is affected by four factors:

▶ **Births and immigration** increase the population.

▶ **Deaths and emigration** decrease the population.

Natural change is the number of births minus the number of deaths. **Net migration** is the number immigrating into a country minus the number emigrating from it.

The UK's population grew from 37m. in 1901 to 61m. today and should reach 71m. by 2031. Growth has been mostly due to natural change rather than net migration.

Births

There are two measures of births – birth rate and total fertility rate.

The birth rate is the number of live births per 1,000 of the population per year.

▶ There has been a long-term decline in the birth rate. In 1900, it was almost 29. By 2007, it had fallen by more than 60%, to under 11.

▶ But there have been fluctuations. There were three 'baby booms': after the two world wars, and in the 1960s. The rate fell sharply in the 1970s, rose during the1980s and early 1990s, and then fell until the recent increase since 2001.

Analysis
Family size doesn't just depend on the number of children – e.g. divorce divides a family into two smaller ones and reduces the chances of the woman having more children.

The total fertility rate is the average number of children a woman will have during her fertile years (aged 15-44). In the 1960s baby boom, it reached an average of 2.95 children per woman, declining to an all-time low of 1.63 in 2001, before rising slightly to 1.84 in 2006. The total fertility rate obviously affects family and household size – the more children a woman has, the bigger the family.

Two important trends are:

▶ More women are remaining childless nowadays.

▶ Women are having children later: the average age is now almost 30.

Reasons for the fall in birth rate

Many social, economic, legal and technological factors are responsible for the falling birth rate and total fertility rate.

1 Changes in the position of women

▶ Increased educational opportunities

▶ More women working

Analysis
Explain *how* such factors affect the birth rate – e.g. 'Better-educated women have more options: they can choose a career rather than marriage and family'.

▶ Changes in attitudes to family life and women's role

▶ Easier access to divorce

▶ Access to abortion and contraception.

2 Fall in the infant mortality rate

The infant mortality rate (IMR) is the number of infants who die before their first birthday, per 1,000 babies born alive, per year. The IMR has fallen greatly in the last century. In 1900, it was 154; by 2007, it was 5. A fall in the IMR may cause a fall in the birth rate: if infants survive, parents will have fewer of them.

Reasons for the fall in the IMR include improved housing, sanitation, nutrition, including that of mothers, knowledge of hygiene and child health, and health services for mothers and children. Medical factors did not play much part until the 1950s, when the IMR began to fall due to mass immunisation, antibiotics, and improved midwifery and obstetrics.

3 Children as an economic liability

Until the late 19th century, children were an economic asset because they went to work from an early age. Now they are an economic liability:

▶ **Laws banning child labour** and introducing compulsory schooling mean they remain economically dependent for longer.

▶ **Changing norms** about children's right to a high standard of living raises their cost.

As a result, parents may be unable to afford to have a large family.

Application
Use your knowledge of the social construction of childhood (Topic 2) to show how the factors that created modern childhood also lead to smaller families.

4 Child-centredness

Childhood is now socially constructed as a uniquely important period and this has led to a shift from 'quantity' to 'quality': parents now have fewer children and lavish more attention and resources on these few.

Effects of a falling birth rate

Lower birth rates and fertility rates have several effects on the family and society – e.g. having fewer children means women are freer to go out to work, creating the dual earner couple.

The dependency ratio is the relationship between the size of the working population and the size of the non-working (dependent) population.

▶ The working population's earnings and taxes support the dependent population.

▶ Children are a large part of the dependent population, so fewer children reduces the 'burden of dependency' on the working population.

Public services Fewer schools and child health services may be needed, and less needs to be spent on maternity and paternity leave. However, these are political decisions – e.g. government can choose either to reduce the number of schools or to have smaller class sizes instead.

Interpretation
Be clear about the difference between *rates* and *numbers* or totals. Rates are always 'out of' something (usually 1,000). The death rate fell despite the number staying constant, because population grew.

Deaths

▶ **The *number* of deaths** has been fairly stable since 1900 (about 600,000 per year), but there have been fluctuations, e.g. the two world wars and the 1918 flu epidemic.

▶ **The death *rate*** is the number of deaths per thousand of the population per year. It has almost halved from 19 in 1900, down to 10 by 2007.

The death rate began falling from about 1870, continuing until 1930. It rose slightly during the 1930s and 1940s due to economic depression and World War Two. Since the 1950s it has declined slightly.

Reasons for the fall in the death rate

Up to 1970, about three-quarters of the decline was due to a fall in deaths from infectious diseases such as TB, measles, smallpox, diarrhoea and typhoid. This decline was largely brought about by changing social factors, including:

Improved nutrition According to McKeown (1972), better diet accounted for half the reduction in the death rate, by increasing people's resistance to infection.

Medical improvements Before the 1950s, medical improvements played almost no part in reducing deaths from infection. From the 1950s, the death rate fell due partly to medical factors such as vaccination, antibiotics, blood transfusion, better maternity services and the creation of the NHS (1949).

Public health improvements More effective government with the power to pass and enforce laws led to improved public health – e.g. better housing, purer drinking water and cleaner air, laws against the adulteration of food and improved sewage disposal.

Other social changes that reduced the death rate include: the decline of more dangerous manual occupations, e.g. mining; smaller families reduced the transmission of infection; greater public knowledge of the causes of illness and higher incomes.

Life expectancy

Life expectancy refers to how long on average a person born in a given year can expect to live. Life expectancy has greatly increased since 1900:

▶ For babies born in 1900 it was 50 years for males, 57 for females.

▶ For babies born in 2005 it was 77 years for males, 81 for females.

Falling infant mortality Low life expectancy in 1900 was largely due to the high IMR pulling down the average life expectancy of the population as a whole. As the IMR fell, life expectancy rose.

The ageing population

The UK population is ageing. In 1971, the average age was 34 years; it is now nearly 40. By 2031, it will reach 42.6. The number of over-65s will overtake the number of under-16s for the first time ever in 2014. There are three main reasons for this ageing:

▶ **Increasing life expectancy** – people are living longer.

▶ **Low infant mortality** – babies no longer die in large numbers.

▶ **Declining fertility** – fewer young people are being born.

Effects of an ageing population

An ageing population has several social and economic effects:

▶ **Public services** Older people consume more health and social care services.

▶ **More one-person pensioner households** These now account for one in every seven households.

▶ **The rising dependency ratio** The non-working old need to be provided for by those of working age, e.g. through taxation to pay for pensions and health care. As the number of retired people rises, the dependency ratio increases.

▶ **Ageism** Age statuses are socially constructed. Old age is often constructed as a problem. Negative stereotyping often portrays the old as incompetent and a burden. (Contrast this with traditional societies, where ageing brings higher status, not lower.)

Policy implications Hirsch (2005) argues that we will need new policies to finance a longer old age. This could be done either by paying more in taxes or by raising the retirement age, or both – e.g. the increase in women's pensionable age from 60 to 65.

Migration

Migration is the movement of people. It can be internal (within a country) or international. Migration affects the size and age structure of the population. Until the 1980s, more people left the UK than entered it.

Immigration

From 1900 to the 1940s, the largest immigrant groups in the UK were the Irish, European Jews and people of British descent from Canada and the USA. Very few immigrants were non-white.

White and non-white immigrants During the 1950s-70s, non-white immigrants began to come from the Caribbean, Africa and South Asia. By 2001, minority ethnic groups accounted for 7.9% of the population. However, most immigrants to the UK were white Irish and Europeans.

Despite this, immigration and nationality acts from 1962 to 1990 placed severe restrictions on non-white immigration. By the 1980s, non-whites accounted for barely a quarter of immigrants. The mainly white countries of the European Union (EU) became the chief source of immigrants.

Emigration

Since 1900, most emigrants have gone to the USA, Canada, Australia, New Zealand and South Africa. The main reasons for emigrating have been economic:

▶ **'Push' factors**, e.g. unemployment and economic recession

▶ **'Pull' factors**, e.g. higher wages or better opportunities.

Application
If a question asks about the consequences of migration, discuss the impact of immigration on family diversity – e.g. Asian extended families and black lone parent families.

Evaluation
Assess the importance of economic factors by referring to the role of non-economic reasons for migrating – e.g. to flee political or ethnic persecution.

ONE TO TRY

Read item A and answer the question that follows.

Item A
Population change comes about because of the combined effects of the rates of births, deaths, emigration and immigration. This can result in a population growing or shrinking, and becoming younger or older.

Economic factors are a major cause of changes in birth and death rates, and in migration patterns. For example, industrialisation led to a fall in the death rate, while a recession may cause people to postpone having a child. However, sociologists argue that many other social, legal and technological factors may also affect population change.

Question Using material from **Item A** and elsewhere, assess the view that population change in the UK since 1900 has been the result of economic factors.
(24 marks)

Examiner's Advice Make sure you use material from Item A. For example, it indicates you should consider birth, death, immigration and emigration in relation to economic factors. These could include job opportunities and economic migrants, the effects on births and deaths of income levels and state welfare spending (inc. funding health services), children as economic assets or liabilities etc. You can evaluate by considering the social, legal and technological factors mentioned in the Item, e.g. the changing position of women, compulsory schooling, availability of contraception etc.

5 Changing Patterns and Family Diversity

Key Issues
▶ What have been the main changes in family patterns in the last 50 years, in terms of partnerships, childbearing and parenting?
▶ What factors are responsible for these changes?
▶ What are the main sociological views and explanations of family diversity?

Interpretation
Questions on the increase in divorce often specify a time period – e.g. 'since 1969'. If so, don't go back to the 1940s – or to the 19th century!

Divorce

40% of marriages now end in divorce – six times more than 50 years ago. There are several reasons for this increase.

Legal changes

Divorce is not the only solution to an unhappy marriage, e.g. 'empty shell' marriage, desertion and legal separation are all alternatives. In the 19th century, divorce was almost impossible. In the 20th century, legal changes made divorce easier: equalising the grounds between the sexes (1923); widening the grounds, e.g. 1969 'irretrievable breakdown', and cheaper divorce, e.g. 1949 legal aid was introduced.

Evaluation
Although the law gives people more freedom to divorce, this doesn't explain why more choose to *exercise* this freedom. Social factors may be more important than legal ones.

Less stigma

Stigma is a negative label. In the past, divorce was stigmatised, e.g. most churches condemned it. However, since the 1960s, this stigma has declined rapidly. This has made divorce more acceptable, so couples are more willing to divorce to solve their problems. Also, because divorce is now more common, this normalises it, thus further reducing the stigma.

Analysis
This means churches' opposition to divorce carries less weight. Also, some churches are now more tolerant of divorce.

Secularisation

Secularisation is the decline in the influence of religion on society. According to Wilson, religious institutions and ideas are losing influence – e.g. church attendance, weddings etc have been declining steadily.

Higher expectations of marriage

Functionalists such as Fletcher (1966) argue that higher expectations of marriage today are leading to higher divorce rates. This is linked to the ideology of romantic love: marriage is now based purely on love, not duty or economic factors as it was in the past. If love dies, there is no longer any reason to stay together. In the past, individuals had little choice about marriage. The family was the unit of production, so marriages took place for economic reasons. People thus had lower expectations and were not dissatisfied by the absence of love, so divorce was less common.

Functionalists are optimistic. They argue that the high rate of re-marriage shows divorcees haven't rejected marriage as such.

Evaluation
Feminists argue that functionalists fail to explain why it's mainly *women* who seek divorce – i.e. because of dissatisfaction with patriarchal oppression.

Changes in women's position

More women are now in paid work, and lone parent welfare benefits are available. This makes women less economically dependent on their husbands and more able to afford divorce.

Women becoming wage-earners also creates a new source of marital conflict. At work, women are increasingly likely to be treated equally – whereas at home they are expected to perform a triple shift (see Topic 1). The resulting awareness of patriarchal oppression at home may result in divorce and explain why 70% of divorce petitions come from women.

Interpretation
If a question asks about couples or partnerships, discuss cohabitation and civil partnerships as well as marriage. If it's about marriage, discuss both first marriages and re-marriages.

Partnerships

Marriage

There are now fewer first marriages, due to several reasons:

▶ **Changing attitudes** mean there is less pressure to marry.

▶ **Alternatives** such as cohabitation are less stigmatised.

▶ **Women's economic independence** gives them freedom not to marry.

▶ **The impact of feminism** means some women see marriage as a patriarchal institution.

▶ **Rising divorce rates** may put some off marrying.

Other trends in marriages include:

▶ **More re-marriages** More divorce means more divorcees available to re-marry, giving rise to serial monogamy.

▶ **Later marriages** The young now spend longer in education and also now cohabit first.

▶ **Fewer church weddings** due to secularisation and some churches not marrying divorcees.

Cohabitation 1.5 million couples in England and Wales cohabit. This is due to less stigma attaching to sex outside marriage, and women's improved economic position – they don't need the financial security of marriage. Cohabitation may be:

▶ **Trial marriage** Cohabitation before marriage is now the norm.

▶ **An alternative to marriage** Couples who see marriage as patriarchal may opt for cohabitation as a more equal relationship.

Analysis
Although new forms of relationship seem to create greater family diversity, you could argue that these look increasingly similar to marriage – e.g. civil partnership gives similar legal rights.

Civil partnerships and same-sex relationships There is now greater acceptance, moves towards legal equality (e.g. civil partnerships) and policies treating all couples (gay or straight) more equally (e.g. in terms of adoption rights). Weeks (1999) argues that acceptance is leading to more stable relationships among gays.

Parenting

Over 40% of children are now born outside marriage – five times more than in 1971. The main reason is the increase in cohabitation. Most births are jointly registered by both parents.

Women are having children later. More are remaining childless, or having fewer children, mainly because they now have more options, e.g. a career.

Lone parent families

These account for a quarter of all families. Numbers have tripled since the 1970s, due to increased divorce and the decline in stigma of births outside marriage. However, the New Right blame generous welfare benefits for encouraging the increase and creating a 'dependency culture'. Over 90% are female-headed, due to the belief that women are suited to the expressive role and to courts giving mothers custody.

Evaluation
Benefits are low, not generous. These families are usually poor, because lack of affordable childcare prevents mothers working and because fathers don't pay maintenance.

Reconstituted or stepfamilies are increasing due to divorce and re-marriage. They now account for 8% of all families with children. These are mostly children from the woman's previous relationship. Stepfamilies are at higher risk of poverty because they have more children, and may also have to support children from a previous relationship.

Ethnic differences

The main ethnic differences in family patterns are:

▶ **More black lone parents** (49% of families) than white (23%) or Asian (11%). This may be the legacy of slavery, the result of high male unemployment, or black women valuing independence more highly.

▶ **Larger Asian households**, due to the cultural importance of the extended family and need for support when migrating. (However, most Asian households are actually nuclear.)

Perspectives on family diversity

Changing family patterns are leading to greater family diversity – a wider range of family types, rather than just the dominance of the nuclear family. There are different perspectives on the extent and importance of family diversity.

> **Interpretation**
> If asked about the extent of and reasons for family diversity, outline the different family types found today. Then examine the causes of diversity, linking these to different perspectives where possible.

Functionalism and the New Right

Functionalism is a modernist sociological perspective. It sees the conventional nuclear family, with a division of labour based on biological differences between the husband's instrumental role and the wife's expressive role, as uniquely suited to the needs of modern industrial society and of family members (see Topic 1).

The New Right is more a political than a sociological perspective. It has had considerable influence on government policies (see Topic 6). It takes a conservative view of the family and opposes diversity. It sees the conventional nuclear family as the only normal or 'natural' one.

Other family types are seen as unnatural and producing social problems, e.g. lone parent families lack an adult male role model and lead to a dependency culture and delinquency. Generous welfare benefits have encouraged these deviant family types.

> **Evaluation**
> Feminists argue that the nuclear family and its gender roles are not 'natural', but social constructs. They see New Right opposition to diversity as an ideology justifying patriarchal oppression.

Chester: the neo-conventional family

Chester (1985) argues that although there is some increased diversity, the nuclear family remains dominant. The only important change has been *from* the conventional family, with a male breadwinner, *to* the neo-conventional family, where both spouses work (like the symmetrical family).

The nuclear family remains the norm that most people aspire to. Most still marry, bring up their children as a couple and don't divorce. Cohabitation has increased but is a temporary phase; most divorcees re-marry. Many of those not currently in a nuclear family either have been or will be. Statistics on household composition are just a snapshot, so they don't show these changes in individuals' life cycles.

The Rapoports: five types of diversity

Rapoport and Rapoport (1982) disagree with Chester. They see diversity as central to the family today. Unlike the New Right, they see diversity as meeting people's needs, not causing family decline. They identify five types of diversity:

▶ **Organisational** – e.g. joint or segregated conjugal roles.

▶ **Cultural** – e.g. ethnic groups have different family structures.

▶ **Class** – e.g. differences in child-rearing practices.

▶ **Life cycle** differences – e.g. pensioner couples, parents with young children.

▶ **Generational** differences – e.g. in attitudes to cohabitation.

> **Application**
> You can use knowledge of relevant studies to illustrate some of these types – e.g. Young and Willmott or Bott on joint versus segregated conjugal roles.

Evaluation
Postmodernism under-estimates how far inequality and oppression restrict people's choices – e.g. divorce lets women escape oppression, but society is still patriarchal, so they end up low paid and with childcare responsibility.

Analysis
Explain *how* contraception and women's independence increase choice in relationships – e.g. financial independence means they are able to leave if they are unhappy.

Postmodernism and family diversity

▶ Unlike in modern society (where functionalists saw the nuclear family as dominant), in postmodern society, there is no one dominant family type.

▶ This is because there is now more choice in relationships (e.g. we can stay single, cohabit, divorce etc). This is leading to more diverse family structures.

These ideas have influenced sociologists. **Giddens** (1992) argues that contraception and women's independence have brought greater choice and equality to relationships. Rather than a relationship being defined by law or tradition, or as solely for the production of children, couples define it to meet their own needs. This means it only lasts as long as it continues to meet their needs. Thus increased choice brings increased instability.

Ulrich Beck: risk society

Beck (1992) sees society today as 'risk society'. People have more choice, so they are more aware of risks – because making choices involves calculating the risks of different courses of action.

In the past, people had little choice. They were expected to marry and play conventional gender roles in a traditional patriarchal family. Although oppressive, this family provided stability by defining each member's role. But the patriarchal family has now been undermined by:

▶ **Greater gender equality**

▶ **Individualism** Self-interest now governs our actions.

The negotiated family Equality and individualism are creating a new family type – the 'negotiated family', which is not fixed but varies according to its members' wishes. Although it is more equal than the patriarchal family, it is less stable, because:

▶ There is more emphasis on *individuals'* needs not those of the family/couple.

▶ Individuals can leave if their needs are not met, resulting in more divorce, lone parents etc.

Postmodernism versus the New Right

Postmodernists reject the New Right view that the nuclear family is the only genuine family type. They argue that:

▶ Diversity is good because it allows people to choose relationships to meet their own needs and enables women to escape oppression.

▶ 'The family' covers many different forms – whatever arrangements those involved *call* a family *is* a family.

Evaluation
Use these criticisms in your evaluation of the New Right view of diversity.

ONE TO TRY

Question Examine the reasons for changes in the divorce rate in the UK since 1969.
(24 marks)

Examiner's Advice Begin by outlining the main pattern – namely the sixfold rise in the divorce rate – but also refer to who petitions for divorce (70% come from women). You should then examine a range of reasons. Make sure you cover changes in the divorce law (especially irretrievable breakdown as the sole ground for divorce), the decline of stigma attached to divorce, the changes in women's position (especially their greater economic independence and the impact of feminist ideas), the effect of secularisation on attitudes to divorce, and rising expectations of marriage. Give your answer a theoretical context by referring where appropriate to feminism, functionalism and the New Right.

6 Social Policy and the Family

Key Issues

▶ In what ways do social policies affect family life?

▶ What are the main sociological perspectives on social policy and the family and how do they differ?

Social policies are the measures taken by state bodies such as schools and welfare agencies. They are usually based on laws introduced by government.

Laws and policies can have both direct and indirect effects on the family:

▶ **Direct effects** Some policies are aimed specifically at family life – e.g. laws on marriage, divorce, child protection, contraception and abortion.

▶ **Indirect effects** Policies on other social or economic issues also affect the family – e.g. compulsory schooling provides childcare for working parents but also keeps children dependent financially for longer.

Application

In essays on policy, you need to give examples of different policies and how they affect family life – so learn a range of them.

Perspectives on policy and the family

Different perspectives have different views on the relationship between social policy and the family.

Functionalism

Functionalists see society as based on value consensus. The state acts in the interests of the whole of society and its policies benefit everyone. Policies help the family to perform its functions – socialising children, caring for the welfare of its members etc.

Evaluation

Functionalism assumes policies benefit everyone, but feminists argue they benefit only men. It also assumes policies make family life better, but they can also make it worse, e.g. cutting benefits to poor families.

▶ There is a 'march of progress' – policies are gradually improving family life; e.g. the welfare state enables families to look after their members better, through access to the NHS etc.

The New Right

The New Right is a conservative political perspective that opposes state intervention in family life. It has had a major influence on social policy.

▶ It sees the traditional nuclear family as 'natural' and based on a biological division of labour between male breadwinner and female nurturer.

▶ If parents perform these roles properly, the family will be self-reliant, able to socialise children effectively and to care for its members.

▶ It opposes family diversity and sees lone parent and same sex families as damaging to children.

The problem The New Right criticise many welfare policies for undermining the family's self-reliance by providing generous benefits, e.g. to lone parent families.

▶ This results in a 'dependency culture' where individuals depend on the state to support their families.

Evaluation
Feminists criticise New Right views as an attempt to justify the patriarchal nuclear family that oppresses women. They argue that the nuclear family is not 'natural' but socially constructed.

Analysis
You can score analysis marks by showing the similarities and/ or differences between different theories.

Evaluation
Not all policies maintain patriarchy – e.g. women's refuges, laws against rape in marriage. In Sweden, policies treat women as individuals, not dependants.

Interpretation
In essays on how policies affect the family, you need to discuss them in the context of different perspectives.

▷ Murray (1984) sees benefits as 'perverse incentives' rewarding irresponsible behaviour – e.g. if the state provides benefits to lone mothers, some fathers will abandon their families.

The solution The New Right favour cutting welfare spending, especially universal benefits. This will give fathers more incentive to provide for their families. Unlike functionalists, who see policies benefiting the family, the New Right believe that the less families depend on the state, the better.

New Labour

New Labour is a political perspective. Like the New Right, it favours the traditional family as usually the best place to raise children, and prefers means-tested benefits targeted at the poor rather than universal benefits. However, unlike the New Right:

▷ It is more accepting of family diversity – e.g. it introduced the Civil Partnership Act and legislation to allow cohabiting couples to adopt.

▷ It believes some policies can improve family life, e.g. extra benefits for poor families.

Feminism

Feminism is a conflict perspective. It sees society as based on a conflict of interests between men and women. Society is patriarchal – male-dominated.

▷ Social policies often shape or define family life in ways that benefit men and maintain patriarchy, disadvantaging women and maintaining their subordination.

▷ Land (1978) argues that policies often assume the patriarchal family to be the norm. As a result, policies act as a self-fulfilling prophecy, actually helping to reproduce this family type. For example, maternity leave is much longer than paternity leave, reinforcing women's responsibility for childcare.

Marxism

Marxism is a conflict perspective. It sees society as divided into two classes, in which the capitalist class exploit the working class by paying them less than the value of what they produce. All social institutions – including policies – serve the interests of capitalism, e.g. the low level of benefits for the old maintains on the cheap those who can no longer be used to produce profits.

Policies affecting families often result from the needs of capitalism. For example:

▷ In World War Two, women were needed as a reserve army of labour and so the government set up nurseries to enable them to work.

▷ After the war, women were no longer needed and the nurseries were closed, forcing them back into the housewife role and dependence on their husbands.

This shows how policies serve the needs of capitalism and how this may affect families.

ONE TO TRY

Question Examine the ways in which social policy can influence families and households. (24 marks)

Examiner's Advice Consider a range of social policies and laws that may affect families. Look at the question from different perspectives, since these have different views on the role of policies in relation to family life. You could consider how far policies maintain inequality within families. A good way to gain marks for evaluation is to create a debate between different perspectives (e.g. New Right versus feminist). The question mentions 'households' so say something about non-family set-ups. Remember that policies (e.g. educational) can affect families indirectly as well as directly.

Practice question and student answer

Read Item A and answer the question that follows.

Item A

Some sociologists argue that there are major inequalities of power and control in modern family relationships.

However, other sociologists argue that roles and relationships in the family are gradually becoming more equal. They argue that attitudes and values are slowly changing. For example, men are now more willing to do housework than they were in the past. This may be linked to women's increased participation in paid work outside the home. For example, one study found that men undertook more domestic labour if their wives were working full-time.

Question

Using material from **Item A** and elsewhere, assess the view that gender roles and relationships in the family are becoming more equal today.

(24 marks)

Student Answer by Floyd

As Item A states, many sociologists today argue that family roles and relationships are gradually becoming more and more equal. For example, Willmott and Young claim that the family is now symmetrical, where husbands now help with the housework and wives go out to work. This is also known as joint conjugal roles, where the couple don't have a fixed division of labour.

> It would be better to take a wider view of the question first – it's not just about housework, but also about power and control in relationships. Also, Floyd could analyse the reasons why the family is now symmetrical.

Willmott and Young argue that the symmetrical family is steadily replacing the old pattern of segregated conjugal roles, which is similar to Parsons' functionalist idea of instrumental and expressive roles. This is where the husband performs the breadwinner (instrumental) role and the wife has the nurturing and caring (expressive) role. According to Parsons, this is based on biological differences between the sexes, a view that the New Right also agree with. However, this can be criticised using Willmott and Young's finding, which shows that men are now doing housework and women are going out to work.

> Accurate and appropriate use of relevant concepts. You could use Willmott and Young to make the evaluation point that this shows family roles are socially constructed and hence not fixed.

However, Willmott and Young have themselves been criticised by feminists such as Anne Oakley. Oakley found that Willmott and Young's study was methodologically flawed. For example, they claimed that 72% of men now helped with the housework, but their definition of the husband helping could be doing as little as putting the rubbish out once a week, or ironing his own shirt. Oakley's own study found that only a small minority of men did a significant amount of housework or childcare.

> Accurate – but avoid writing any more than Floyd does here on this rather dated material.

> Good analytical point about women being responsible. You could link it to the idea that men merely 'help'.

Oakley's findings are backed up by Mary Boulton, who argues that we need to look not just at who does what around the house, but who takes responsibility for it. Boulton claims that although men may do some domestic tasks, responsibility e.g. for getting the food on the table or ensuring the children go to school clean still lies with the woman.

> Gershuny brings things more up to date and shifts attention to the impact of women's paid work – but Floyd needs to broaden his answer to include power and control issues too.

However, as Item A points out, attitudes and values are changing so many men now feel it is right that they should do more housework, especially if their wives work full-time. Gershuny found that there was a cultural lag and that couples were now 'catching up' to the fact that men need to do more because so many women now go out to work.

> A good account of feminist criticisms and two useful concepts – but still focused on domestic roles. Floyd also needs a separate final paragraph drawing conclusions from his answer.

However, this view has been criticised by feminists. They argue that in reality women who work face a 'double burden' – they have to go out to work, yet still do the majority of the housework when they come home. Dunscombe and Marsden go further and claim that these women work a 'triple shift'. Not only are they responsible for housework and paid work, they also have to perform 'emotion work', managing the feelings of the rest of the family. This supports the view in Item A that there are still major inequalities in family relationships.

$\frac{16}{24}$

How to turn this into a top-mark answer

This is a reasonably good answer that gets fairly close to the top mark band. With some further work, it could be turned into a full-mark answer. It already has a fair amount of explicit evaluation of the different arguments and evidence it presents, and it analyses the issues reasonably well. The material used is relevant and is applied appropriately. However, there are several things Floyd could do to boost his marks further.

Interpretation and application

Floyd interprets the question as being about men and women's roles in the domestic division of labour and then does a good job of explaining the debates about this aspect of family roles, including how far women's paid work affects the division of labour in the home. However, he says nothing about other aspects, which are more about 'the relationships' referred to in the question and the 'inequalities of power and control' mentioned in Item A. To get into the top band, you need to look at issues such as domestic violence, control of family resources and decision making. For full marks, you need to discuss some of these in detail, and probably therefore spend less time on the domestic division of labour, especially the older studies.

Concepts and theories

Floyd uses a range of concepts appropriately and generally defines or explains them – e.g. division of labour, joint and segregated conjugal roles, instrumental and expressive roles, cultural lag, dual burden and triple shift. However, a serious omission is the feminist concept of patriarchy, which should be central to this answer – especially in relation to domestic violence, resources and decision making. The idea of 'march of progress' theories could also be used, e.g. to link Willmott and Young to Gershuny.

Studies

Several studies of domestic labour are used, though some are rather dated. There are none on power and control. You could use Dobash and Dobash on domestic violence, Kempson or Pahl and Vogler on resources, and Edgell on decision making.

CHAPTER 2 EDUCATION

1 Class Differences in Achievement

Key Issues

▶ What are the patterns of achievement in relation to social class?

▶ What is the role of different home background factors in causing class differences in achievement?

▶ How do factors and processes in schools contribute to these differences?

Class patterns of achievement

Working-class pupils in general achieve less than middle-class pupils in education. For example, children of higher professionals are 2-3 times more likely than children of routine manual workers to get five or more A*-C grades at GCSE, and about five times more likely to go to university. Sociologists have put forward a range of explanations for these differences, which can be divided into:

▶ **External or home background factors** that lie outside the school.

▶ **Internal factors** within the school and the education system.

Achievement and home background

Class differences in pupils' home background may play a key role in causing differences in achievement. Home background includes many things, but these can be grouped into two different types of factor:

▶ **Cultural factors** These include class differences in norms and values acquired through socialisation, attitudes to education, speech codes etc.

▶ **Material factors** These are the physical necessities of life, such as adequate housing, diet and income.

Interpretation
Be very clear about these two terms, because questions sometimes ask you to define or give examples of one or other of them.

Cultural deprivation theory

The main cultural explanation for class differences in achievement is cultural deprivation theory.

▶ 'Culture' refers to all the norms, values, beliefs, skills and knowledge that a society or a group regards as important. This culture is transmitted to the next generation through socialisation.

▶ Different classes socialise their children differently and this may affect their achievement.

▶ According to cultural deprivation theory, some working-class parents fail to transmit the appropriate norms, values, attitudes, knowledge, skills etc – that is, the 'right' culture – needed for educational success.

Cultural deprivation theorists see three factors as responsible for working-class under-achievement: **a lack of intellectual stimulation, the restricted speech code** and **working-class subculture**.

Intellectual stimulation

Working-class parents are less likely to give their children educational toys and activities that will stimulate their thinking and reasoning skills, and less likely to read to them. This affects their intellectual development so that when they begin school they are at a disadvantage compared with middle-class children.

Speech codes

Basil Bernstein (1975) distinguishes between elaborated and restricted speech codes.

▶ **The working class use the restricted code.** This is less analytic and more descriptive, has a limited vocabulary and is formed of simple sentences or even just gestures. It is particularistic – it assumes that the listener shares the particular meanings that the speaker holds, so the speaker doesn't spell them out.

▶ **The middle class use the elaborated code.** This is more analytic, with a wide vocabulary and complex sentences. It is universalistic – speakers spell out their meanings explicitly and don't just assume the listener shares them.

Crucially, the elaborated code is the one used in education, by teachers, exams, textbooks, university interviewers etc. This gives the middle class an educational advantage.

Working-class subculture

Cultural deprivation theorists identify three aspects of working-class subculture that contribute to under-achievement:

▶ **Immediate gratification** Wanting rewards now rather than being willing to make sacrifices and working hard for future rewards – unlike the deferred gratification practised by the middle class.

▶ **Fatalism** A belief that 'whatever will be, will be'. Working-class children don't believe they can improve their position through their own individual efforts.

▶ **Low value on education** Hyman argues that the working class don't value education (and don't believe they will benefit from it), so they don't try. Douglas argues that working-class parents show less interest in their children's education and give them less support; e.g. they are less likely than middle-class parents to attend parents' evenings.

Criticisms of cultural deprivation theory

▶ It ignores the importance of material factors such as poverty.

▶ It ignores the impact of school factors, e.g. negative labelling by teachers.

▶ It blames the victim for their failure. Critics argue that the working class are not culturally deprived – they simply have a different culture from the school and this puts them at a disadvantage.

Material deprivation

Material deprivation or poverty can cause working-class under-achievement because of factors such as:

▶ **Poor housing** Overcrowding or cold and damp rooms mean pupils have nowhere quiet to do homework. Similarly, being homeless or living in temporary accommodation may mean frequent moves and changes of school.

▶ **Poor diet** can lead to illness, absences from school and lack of concentration in class due to hunger.

Analysis
Explaining how these three factors might be linked to each other will gain you marks.

Analysis
Explain the meaning of the two codes, and then explain why the elaborated code is used in education – e.g. 'Textbooks use it because they don't know who their readers are, so they have to spell out their meanings very explicitly in a way that will be understood 'universally' – i.e. by everyone'.

Evaluation
Critics argue that working-class parents don't attend parents' evenings because they work longer hours, or because they feel inferior to the teachers – not because they aren't interested in their children's education.

Evaluation
Not all poor children fail – those with supportive parents may have high levels of motivation. Material deprivation theory also ignores factors in school such as teacher labelling and streaming, which may cause under-achievement.

Low income Such problems are often caused by low income. This can affect educational achievement in several ways, e.g.:

▶ Lack of educational materials – books, PC with internet access etc.

▶ Lack of the right uniform or the latest fashion items, which can lead to bullying.

▶ Not being able to afford university fees.

Cultural capital theory

This approach combines aspects of both cultural and material explanations. Marxists such as Bourdieu (1984) argue that middle-class pupils are more successful than working-class pupils because their parents possess more capital or assets. This capital comes in two forms:

▶ **Economic capital** The wealth that middle-class families own

▶ **Cultural capital** The attitudes, values, skills, knowledge etc of the middle class.

Educational capital The middle class use their greater economic and cultural capital to give their children an advantage by using it to obtain educational capital – qualifications. This allows their children to get middle-class jobs and more economic capital, thus reproducing the advantages of the middle class from generation to generation.

School factors and achievement

Factors and processes within schools and the education system also influence class differences in achievement. Most sociologists who have studied the role of school factors are interactionists who focus on small-scale interactions between teachers and pupils. They identify a number of related causes of under-achievement: **labelling; the self-fulfilling prophecy; streaming** and **pupil subcultures**.

Labelling

Labels are meanings or definitions we attach to someone or something to make sense of them – e.g. middle-class pupils are labelled 'bright, 'motivated', 'cooperative' etc. Becker (1961) argues that teachers label middle-class children as 'ideal pupils' and prefer to teach them rather than working-class children.

The key idea of labelling underlies many of the other processes within schools that cause under-achievement.

The self-fulfilling prophecy

A prophecy is a prediction made about something or someone (e.g. "he's stupid – he's bound to fail"). The key feature of a *self-fulfilling* prophecy is that it comes true simply because it has been made (e.g. he goes on to fail all his exams).

Teachers can create self-fulfilling prophecies through the labels they attach to pupils. Studies of labelling show that 'what teachers believe, pupils achieve'. That is, while teachers believe middle-class pupils to be bright (and therefore succeed), working-class pupils are likely to be labelled negatively and thus fail.

Streaming

Streaming is an extreme and institutionalised form of labelling. It works by putting all pupils of similar ability together into the same class or 'stream' for all subjects: 'bright' pupils are grouped together in the top stream, 'thick' ones in the bottom. Lacey (1970) describes streaming as 'differentiation' – a way of separating the sheep from the goats and then educating them differently. Streaming often creates a self-fulfilling prophecy:

In questions on differences
in achievement, you need
to apply this by noting
that working-class pupils
end up in lower streams
and middle-class pupils
in higher ones because
of teacher labelling, thus
widening the achievement
gap between the classes.

▶ Douglas found that the IQ of pupils labelled as less able and placed in the bottom stream, actually *fell* over time, whereas that of pupils put in the top stream *increased*.

▶ Those placed in lower streams may be denied access to the same curriculum – e.g. not being put in for higher level exams.

Pupil subcultures

A subculture is a group whose beliefs, values and attitudes differ to some extent from the culture of wider society. Pupils may form their own subcultures in response to labelling:

▶ **Pro-school subcultures** are usually formed by pupils in higher streams. They accept the school's values and goals of hard work, regular attendance, respect for teachers etc. Typically they enjoy school, participate enthusiastically in its activities and intend to continue in education.

▶ **Anti-school subcultures** are often formed by those in lower streams. They reject the school's values and often invert them (turn them upside down). They dislike school, flout its rules, disrespect teachers, avoid doing schoolwork, play truant, sabotage their uniform etc.

Status and subcultures Lacey argues that lower-stream pupils form or join anti-school subcultures because school deprives them of status by labelling them as failures. Therefore these pupils create their own status hierarchy: they gain status from their peers by rejecting the school's values and breaking its rules.

Pupil subcultures often lead to a self-fulfilling prophecy: members of pro-school subcultures work hard and are successful, while those in anti-school subcultures mess about, truant and fail.

Educational policies

What goes on in schools isn't just a product of what teachers decide to do. It is also greatly influenced by government policies, and these can have an important effect on class differences in achievement. For example, some sociologists argue that marketisation policies have increased the amount of streaming in schools.

Likewise, policies on issues such as grants, fees, maintenance allowances, the school leaving age, compensatory education etc have an impact on home background factors such as material or cultural deprivation.

Evaluation
Focusing on internal factors may mean we neglect the role of home background factors such as poverty and cultural deprivation. An adequate account of under-achievement needs to take these into consideration too.

Interpretation
If a question asks about factors *in schools*, focus on labelling, the self-fulfilling prophecy, streaming and pupil subcultures. If it asks about factors *in the education system*, talk about policies as well (see Topic 6).

ONE TO TRY

Question Outline some of the causes of class differences in educational achievement. (12 marks)

Examiner's Advice There are 8 marks for your knowledge of causes of under-achievement but also 4 marks for explaining or assessing them. You should include different types of factors, including both internal ones such as labelling and pupil subcultures and external or home background factors. On the latter, you should refer to both cultural and material factors. You don't have time to go into detail on all these, so pick three or four (e.g. pupil subcultures, material deprivation, cultural deprivation and cultural capital) and write a paragraph on each one. To get into the higher mark ranges, you need to explain why each of these factors may lead to class differences in achievement, e.g. middle-class parents have more cultural capital, which means they know how the education system works and can use this to get their children into better schools.

2 Ethnic Differences in Achievement

Key Issues
▶ What are the patterns of achievement in relation to different ethnic groups?
▶ What influence do external cultural and material factors have on these patterns?
▶ How far are differences in achievement due to racism inside schools and the education system?

What is an ethnic group?
▶ Ethnicity refers to a shared culture, identity and history. An ethnic group is a group of people who see themselves as a distinct group based for example on religion, geography or language.

▶ An ethnic minority group may be of a different skin colour from the majority population, but not necessarily so.

▶ However, in the case of Britain, the largest minority groups are non-white: mainly of African, Caribbean or South Asian origin.

▶ Deciding who is in which ethnic group is a problem. Should all 'Asians' be classified together when this covers many different nationalities, religions and languages?

Ethnic differences in achievement
Patterns of ethnic achievement are complex, cross-cut by gender and social class. For example:

▶ Black, Pakistani and Bangladeshi pupils do worst; Indians do best.

▶ White pupils are very close to the national average, but this is because they form the great majority of the school population.

▶ Among white and black working-class pupils, girls do better than boys, but among Asians, boys do better than girls.

▶ Working-class black girls do better than working-class white girls.

Explaining differences in achievement
There are two sets of factors:

▶ **Internal factors** within schools and the education system, e.g. pupil-teacher interaction and educational policies.

▶ **External factors** outside the education system, e.g. home and family background.

External factors and ethnic differences

The main external factors affecting ethnic differences in achievement are:

▶ **Cultural deprivation**

▶ **Material deprivation and class**

▶ **Racism in wider society**

Interpretation
Gender and class differences exist within and between ethnic groups. Remember that everyone has a class, an ethnicity and a gender, and their achievement is affected by the interplay of all three.

Application
When answering essay questions on ethnicity and achievement, refer to the achievement patterns of a range of different ethnic groups.

Analysis
Distinguish clearly between these three explanations to gain marks for 'unpacking' the idea of external factors.

Cultural deprivation

Cultural deprivation theory claims that the under-achievement of some ethnic groups is caused by inadequate socialisation in the home. This explanation has two main aspects:

▶ **Intellectual and language skills**

▶ **Attitudes, values and family structure.**

Intellectual and language skills

▶ Cultural deprivation theory claims that children from low-income black families lack intellectual stimulation. As a result, they fail to develop reasoning and problem-solving skills.

▶ Bereiter and Engelmann claim that the language of poorer black American families is ungrammatical and disjointed. As a result, their children are unable to express abstract ideas – a major barrier to educational progress.

▶ Some claim that children who do not speak English at home may be held back educationally.

Attitudes, values and family structure

Differences in attitudes and values towards education may be the result of differences in socialisation. Most children are socialised into the mainstream culture, which instils competitiveness and a desire to achieve, thus equipping them for success in education.

▶ **Fatalism and immediate gratification** Cultural deprivation theorists claim that the subculture into which some black children are socialised is fatalistic and focused on immediate gratification, resulting in a lack of motivation to succeed.

▶ **The lack of a male role model** at home for many African-Caribbean boys may encourage them to turn to an anti-educational macho 'gang culture'. The New Right thinker Murray (1984) argues that the high rate of lone parenthood and a lack of positive male role models lead to the under-achievement of some minority pupils.

▶ **Culture of poverty** Moynihan (1965) argues that the absence of a male role model of achievement in black matrifocal lone parent families produces inadequately socialised children who fail at school, become inadequate parents themselves and perpetuate a culture of poverty.

▶ **The impact of slavery** Pryce (1979) argues that Black Caribbean culture is less resistant to racism because of the experience of slavery. As a result, many black pupils have low self-esteem and under-achieve.

▶ **Asian families** Most studies focus on supposedly dysfunctional black families, but Khan (1979) argues that the Asian family is an obstacle to achievement, especially for girls, because it takes a controlling attitude towards them. As a result they do less well than boys.

White working-class pupils

Most research has focused on ethnic minority families, but white working-class pupils also under-achieve. This may be because they have lower aspirations than many other ethnic groups and this may be the result of white working-class culture, including a lack of parental support. There is recent evidence to support this view.

▶ **Lupton** (2004) studied four mainly working-class schools with different ethnic compositions. Teachers reported poorer levels of behaviour and discipline in the white working-class schools, which they linked to lower levels of parental support and the negative attitudes of white working-class parents towards education.

▶ **Evans** (2006) argues that street culture in white working-class areas can be brutal and is brought into school. The result is a strong pressure to reject education.

Evaluation
According to the Swann Report (1985), language is not a major factor in under-achievement. Any negative effect is likely to be temporary. Indian pupils do well despite often not speaking English at home.

Evaluation
Evidence contradicting this view comes from Connor (2004), who found that minority ethnic parents often place a higher value on education than white parents, and Sewell (1998), who found that only a minority of African-Caribbean boys were anti-school.

Evaluation
Some argue that Asian families have more positive attitudes towards education and that adult authority in them is similar to that in schools, so that Asian parents are more likely than white parents to support the school's behaviour policies.

Interpretation
When answering a question on ethnicity and achievement, don't just refer to non-white pupils. Referring to white working-class under-achievement provides balance in your answer.

Compensatory education

Compensatory education is an educational policy that aims to counter the effects of cultural deprivation, e.g.:

▶ **Operation Head Start** in the USA was established to compensate children for the cultural deficit they are said to suffer because of deprived backgrounds.

▶ **Sure Start** in the UK aims to support the development of pre-school children in deprived areas.

Criticisms of cultural deprivation

Cultural deprivation theory has been widely criticised as an explanation of ethnic differences in achievement:

▶ **Victim-blaming** Keddie argues that it is a victim-blaming explanation. Minority ethnic group children are culturally different, not culturally deprived, and they under-achieve because schools are ethnocentric – biased in favour of white culture.

▶ **Cultural exclusion** Ball argues that minority ethnic group parents are at a disadvantage because they are less aware of how to negotiate the British education system. This results in 'cultural exclusion' rather than cultural deprivation. According to Gewirtz, complex school application forms are an example of cultural exclusion practices in some schools.

▶ **Cultural domination** Compensatory education imposes the dominant white middle-class culture on minority ethnic group pupils' own culture.

Material deprivation and class

Material deprivation (or poverty) is a lack of the physical or economic resources essential for normal life in society. Material deprivation explanations of ethnic differences in achievement argue that educational failure is the result of material factors such as substandard housing and low income. Ethnic minorities are more likely to face these problems. For example, evidence shows that:

▶ Pakistanis and Bangladeshis are much more likely than whites to be poor.

▶ For many minorities, unemployment is higher, pay is lower and overcrowding in the home is more likely.

▶ According to the Swann Report (1985), social class accounts for at least half of the difference in educational achievement between ethnic groups.

▶ The lowest achieving minority ethnic groups are those with the lowest social class position, e.g. Bangladeshi and Pakistani pupils are more likely to be working-class and more likely to do worse compared with Indian and white pupils.

Racism in wider society

While material deprivation among minority ethnic groups clearly affects pupils' achievement, it may itself be the product of racism in wider society. Members of minority ethnic groups face direct and indirect discrimination at work and in the housing market. As a result, they are more likely to have low pay or be unemployed, and this affects their children's educational opportunities.

Racial discrimination in jobs and housing → social exclusion → unemployment, low pay, inadequate housing → affects children's education

Internal factors and ethnic differences

Analysis
Show you know all three and deal with them separately, but also explain how they can be linked together as parts of a whole package of inter-related factors.

Some sociologists focus on the impact of factors within school and the education system as causing ethnic differences in achievement. These internal factors include:

▶ **Labelling**

▶ **Pupil subcultures**

▶ **Ethnocentricity and institutional racism**

Labelling

Application
When describing a factor (such as labelling), make sure you spell out exactly *how* it ultimately leads to educational under-achievement.

Interactionists focus on small-scale, face-to-face interactions, such as those between pupils and teachers. They are interested in the impact of the labels that teachers give to children from different ethnic backgrounds; e.g. black pupils are often seen as disruptive and Asian pupils as passive.

As a result of these negative racist labels, teachers may treat ethnic minority pupils differently, disadvantaging them and bringing about a self-fulfilling prophecy that leads to their under-achievement. Sociologists have studied labelling in relation to both black and Asian pupils.

Evaluation
How can Gillborn and Youdell be sure that the behaviour was only *interpreted* as problematic and wasn't *in fact* misbehaviour? The two are very difficult to separate out.

Black pupils

Gillborn and Youdell (2000) found teachers had 'racialised expectations' (labels) about black pupils and expected more discipline problems and saw their behaviour as threatening. Black pupils were more likely than others to be punished for the same behaviour. The pupils felt that their teachers underestimated their ability and picked on them.

Gillborn and Youdell conclude that conflict between white teachers and black pupils stems from the racist stereotypes that teachers have, rather than from the pupils' actual behaviour. This can cause under-achievement because it leads to:

▶ **Higher levels of exclusions of black boys**

▶ **Black pupils being placed in lower sets or streams.**

Asian pupils

Research on Asian pupils shows evidence of teacher stereotyping:

Wright (1992) found that Asian primary school pupils were stereotyped by their teachers and treated differently:

▶ Teachers assumed the children would have a poor grasp of English and so they used simplistic language when speaking to them.

▶ They mispronounced children's names.

▶ They saw them as a problem that they could ignore.

Analysis
Explain why these teacher actions might reduce pupils' self-esteem and create under-achievement.

As a result, Asian pupils, especially the girls, were marginalised and prevented from participating fully, affecting their self-esteem.

Connolly (1998) found that primary school teachers saw Asian pupils as passive and conformist. Both teachers and pupils saw Asian boys as more 'feminine', vulnerable and less able to protect themselves.

Pupil subcultures

Pupils may react in a variety of different ways to racist labelling in school, including forming or joining pupil subcultures. Sewell (1998) found that black boys adopted a range of responses to teachers' racist labelling of them as rebellious and anti-school.

▶ **Conformists** were the largest group. They were keen to succeed, accepted the school's goals and had friends from different ethnic groups.

▶ **Innovators** were the second largest group. They were pro-education but anti-school. They valued success, but not teachers' approval.

▶ **Retreatists** were a tiny minority of isolated individuals disconnected from both the school and black subcultures outside it.

▶ **Rebels** were a small but highly visible minority of black pupils. They rejected the school's goals and rules and conformed instead to the stereotype of the 'black macho lad'. They despised both white boys and conformist black boys. Their aim was to achieve the status of 'street hood'.

However, despite only a small minority of black boys actually fitting the stereotype of the 'black macho lad', teachers tended to see them all in this way. This resulted in the under-achievement of many boys, not just the rebels, as a result of discrimination by teachers.

Asian boys O'Donnell and Sharpe (2000) found a macho 'warrior' response similar to the 'rebels' among some Asian boys who despised more conformist Asian youths as 'weaklings'.

Rejecting negative labels

Studies show that not all minority ethnic pupils who are negatively labelled accept and conform to the label. Some may remain committed to succeeding despite racist labelling:

▶ **Fuller** (1984) studied a group of high-achieving black girls in year 11 of a London comprehensive. The girls maintained a positive self-image by rejecting teachers' stereotypes of them. They recognised the value of education and were determined to achieve, but only conformed in terms of doing their schoolwork, working hard without giving the appearance of doing so. They didn't seek the teachers' approval, and they maintained friendships with black girls in lower streams. In some ways they are similar to the innovators in Sewell's study.

▶ **Mac an Ghaill's** (1992) study of black and Asian 'A' level students at a sixth form college found that they did not necessarily accept teachers' negative labels – e.g. some girls felt that the all-girls school they had previously attended gave them a greater academic commitment.

However, Mirza (1992) found that black girls' strategies for dealing with teachers' racism, e.g. not asking certain staff for help, sometimes restricted their opportunities. Even though they did not accept the labels, they were still disadvantaged as a result.

Institutional racism

Many sociologists argue that although the racist labelling practised by some teachers is important, it is not an adequate explanation for the widespread ethnic differences found in achievement. Instead, they argue, we must focus on institutional racism – discrimination against ethnic minorities that is built into the way institutions such as schools and colleges operate on a routine or even unconscious basis, rather than the conscious intentions of individual teachers.

The ethnocentric curriculum

This is an important example of institutional racism. 'Ethnocentric' refers to an attitude or policy that prioritises the culture of one particular ethnic group while disregarding or downgrading others. Many sociologists have argued that the curriculum of British schools is ethnocentric.

Evaluation
This tells us the range and characteristics of possible pupil responses, but not why different boys chose different responses.

Interpretation
You can use Sewell's study to show you are aware that pupils' responses to racism in schools vary considerably – not all live up to their teachers' negative expectations.

Evaluation
Use Fuller and Mac an Ghaill's findings to criticise labelling as deterministic – it doesn't inevitably result in a self-fulfilling prophecy of failure.

Evaluation
Although the school curriculum largely ignores Asian culture, Indian and Chinese pupils' achievement is still above average. Also, Stone argues that there is no evidence that black pupils actually suffer from low self-esteem.

- **Troyna and Williams** note that it gives priority to white culture and the English language.
- **David** argues that the National Curriculum is a 'specifically British' curriculum that teaches the culture of the 'host community'.
- **Ball** sees the history curriculum in British schools as recreating a 'mythical age of empire and past glories', while at the same time ignoring the history of black and Asian people.

The result may be that minority ethnic group pupils feel that they and their culture and identity are not valued in education and this diminishes their sense of self-esteem, which has a negative effect on their educational achievement.

Other examples of institutional racism include:

- **Setting and streaming** The CRE (1992) study of 'Jayleigh' school found that Asian pupils were consistently placed in lower sets than their ability warranted and were less likely to be entered for GCSE exams. Similarly, the workings of the 'A*-C economy' meant that black pupils were placed in lower sets and had less chance of gaining qualifications.
- **Governing bodies** Hatcher (1996) found that schools' governing bodies gave a low priority to 'race' issues, failed to deal with racist behaviour and often lacked formal channels of communication with ethnic minority parents. Ranson (2005) found that governing bodies are disproportionately white.

Analysis
Show you know the difference between individual racism (e.g. by teachers) and institutional racism (resulting from the structure of the school/college).

Selection and segregation

The selection procedures followed by schools can also be a form of institutional racism when they are used in a discriminatory way against minority ethnic group pupils.

The Commission for Racial Equality (1993) found racism in secondary schools' admissions procedures, e.g. primary school reports stereotyped minority pupils; there was a lack of information or application forms in minority languages and there was bias in entrance interviews.

Marketisation may make this worse by increasing the amount of selection in the education system and creating more opportunities for negative stereotypes to affect school admissions. This makes it more difficult for some minority pupils to get into high-achieving schools. As a result, the education system becomes racially segregated, with minority pupils more likely to be concentrated in unpopular, unsuccessful schools.

Self-segregation Gewirtz found that Asian parents made active choices to avoid 'rough' schools with a reputation for racism, opting instead for ones they perceived as 'safe' and with firm discipline.

Application
Use examples of policies that promote marketisation (see Topic 6), such as exam league tables, to show how they could lead to increased ethnic segregation as schools filter out minority groups they regard as under-achievers or 'liability' pupils.

ONE TO TRY

Question Outline some of the school factors that may lead to the educational under-achievement of pupils from some minority ethnic groups. (12 marks)

Examiner's Advice There are 8 marks for your knowledge of school factors but also 4 marks for explaining or assessing them. Keep the focus of your answer on school factors such as labelling, teachers' racialised expectations, anti-school pupil subcultures, the ethnocentric curriculum, institutionalised racism etc. To get into the higher mark ranges, you need to explain why each of these factors may lead to the under-achievement of some minority ethnic group pupils, e.g. teachers' racialised expectations may create negative self-images for some pupils which they may then conform to by seeing no point in working. If you refer to non-school factors, only do so as a way of assessing the importance of school factors.

3 Gender Differences in Education

Key Issues
▶ What are the gender patterns in achievement and subject choice?
▶ Why do girls now do better than boys at most subjects and most levels of achievement?
▶ Why do girls and boys choose to study different subjects?
▶ How does schooling help to reinforce gender identities?

Gender patterns in achievement

In the past, boys out-performed girls, but since the 1980s girls have improved more rapidly and now they do better than boys at all levels and in most subjects:

▶ At Key Stages 1 to 3, girls do consistently better than boys, especially in English. In science and maths the gap is narrower.

▶ At GCSE, girls are around 10 percentage points ahead.

▶ At AS and A level, girls are more likely to pass, and to get higher grades, though the gap is narrower than at GCSE

▶ Girls even do better in traditional boys' subjects like sciences.

▶ More girls than boys go into higher education.

Reasons for improvements in girls' achievement

The possible reasons for improvements in girls' educational achievement can be divided into external and internal factors:

▶ **External factors** – factors outside the education system, such as home and family background, the job market and wider society.

▶ **Internal factors** – factors within schools and the education system, such as the effect of schools' equal opportunities policies.

External factors and girls' achievement

Sociologists have identified a range of external factors that have contributed to the improvement in girls' achievement.

The influence of feminism

Since the 1960s, feminists have challenged patriarchy in all areas of social life and rejected the traditional stereotypes of women as inferior to men in the home, work, education and law.

▶ Feminists have had an impact on women's rights and opportunities through campaigns to win changes in the law, e.g. on equal pay, outlawing rape in marriage etc.

▶ More broadly, feminist ideas are likely to have affected girls' self-image and aspirations. As a result, they are more motivated to do well in education.

Girls' changing perceptions and ambitions

Linking to the influence of feminism, studies show that there has been a major shift in how girls see themselves and their future:

Sharpe (1994) compared her two studies of working-class girls in the 1970s and 1990s. She found that:

▶ In the 1970s, girls' priorities were 'love, marriage, husbands, children, jobs and careers, more or less in that order'. They saw their future in terms of a domestic role, not paid work.

▶ In the 1990s, priorities had switched to careers and being able to be independent.

Francis (2001) found that girls now had high career aspirations and so needed educational qualifications.

Changes in the family

There have been major changes in the family since the 1970s:

▶ An increase in the divorce rate – about 40% of marriages now end this way.

▶ More lone parent families, over 90% of which are female headed.

▶ More cohabitation and a decrease in first marriages.

▶ Smaller families and more women staying single.

These changes mean women have both more need and more opportunity to be economically independent – and this gives them more motivation to do well educationally and get good qualifications.

Changes in women's employment

There are now more employment opportunities for women than previously as a result of the expansion of the service sector – traditionally an area of women's work. Women's employment has risen from under half of married women in the 1950s to about three quarters today.

Changes in the law have improved the position of working women:

▶ The 1970 Equal Pay Act and the 1975 Sex Discrimination Act give women more employment rights.

▶ Since 1975, the pay gap between men and women has almost halved.

As a result of these changes, girls today have more incentive to see their future in terms of paid work and this creates an incentive for them to gain qualifications.

Internal factors and girls' achievement

There have been major changes in the education system since the 1970s and some sociologists see these as important in explaining girls' improved performance.

Equal opportunities policies

Feminist ideas are now widespread in the education system. In particular, the basic belief in gender equality and that boys and girls are equally capable and should have the same opportunities is now widely accepted and has become a social norm within education.

Application
Ensure that in describing such studies, you explain how this impacts on girls' attitudes towards and achievement in education.

Interpretation
In discussing these factors, beware of treating the question as if it's about the family and not about education. Keep it linked to girls' achievement!

Analysis
Although for convenience we can divide explanations into internal and external factors, in reality they are linked. Make this analytical point by showing connections between some of these factors.

This has led to policies aimed at giving girls and boys equal opportunities, such as:

▶ **GIST** and **WISE** programmes to encourage girls into science and technology.

▶ **The National Curriculum**, introduced in 1988, means that girls and boys now largely study the same subjects. For example, making science compulsory has helped to equalise opportunities.

Meritocracy As a result of such policies, education is now more meritocratic (based on the principle of equal opportunity). Now that girls have more equal opportunities than in the past, they are able to do better.

Role models

There are now more female teachers and head teachers than in the past and these provide positive, pro-educational role models for girls.

The presence of more female teachers also 'feminises' the learning environment and encourages girls to see school as part of a female 'gender domain'. As a result, they come to perceive educational success as a desirable feminine characteristic.

Coursework

According to Mitsos and Browne (1998), girls do better than boys in coursework, because they are more conscientious and better organised. Girls mature earlier and can concentrate for longer.

As a result, its introduction into the curriculum boosted girls' exam results more than boys'. For example, Gorard (2005) found that the gender gap in achievement increased sharply when GCSE was introduced in 1988, because coursework was a major part of most subjects.

Stereotypes in learning materials

Studies of reading schemes, textbooks and other learning materials have shown that in the past, females were both under-represented and were portrayed as subordinate to males, in domestic roles or unsuited to certain subjects (e.g. science).

However, since the 1980s, many of these sexist images have been removed and replaced with more positive images of females. This may have an impact on girls' perceptions of what women can do and thus may raise their aspirations.

Teacher attention

Earlier studies, e.g. Spender (1983), found that teachers spent more time interacting with boys than with girls. However, more recent studies suggest girls may benefit more than boys:

▶ **French and French** (1993) found that teachers paid boys and girls similar amounts of attention for academic reasons. But boys received more attention overall because they attracted more punishments for misbehaviour.

▶ **Francis** (2001) found that although boys received more attention, they were disciplined more harshly and felt teachers picked on them and had lower expectations of them.

▶ **Swann** (1998) found that boys dominate class discussions whereas girls prefer group work and are better at listening and cooperating. This finds favour with teachers, who respond more positively to girls and give them more encouragement.

Selection and league tables

Marketisation policies such as publication of exam 'league tables' (see Topic 6) have led to competition between schools. Schools have an incentive to try to recruit more able students in order to boost their results and league table position.

Evaluation
Although coursework has some impact on results, Elwood (2005) notes that exams have more influence on final grades, so the introduction of coursework had only limited effect on gender differences in achievement.

Analysis
Link ideas together – e.g. you can connect the removal of stereotypes to equal opportunities policies and the impact of feminist ideas on education.

Analysis
Explain *how* these classroom interaction processes might help girls to do better.

▶ **Girls** are generally more successful than boys, so they are more attractive to schools.

▶ **Boys** are lower-achieving and more badly-behaved (they are four times more likely than girls to be excluded). Schools see them as 'liability students' who will give them a bad image and produce poor results.

As a result, girls are more likely to get places in successful schools. In turn, girls get a better education and achieve more.

Boys' under-achievement

Recently, attention has focused on reasons for boys' under-achievement. Sociologists have identified several factors that may be responsible. Some of these are the 'opposite' of the factors that have led to girls' performance improving, such as the kind of role models in schools or at home, or the jobs available to males and females.

Literacy One reason for boys lagging behind is their poorer literacy skills.

▶ Parents spend less time reading to sons and it is mainly mothers who read to young children and so reading is seen as a feminine activity.

▶ Boys' leisure interests (e.g. sport and computer games) don't encourage language and communication skills, whereas girls' 'bedroom culture' does.

Because language and literacy are important in most subjects, boys' poorer skills have a wide-ranging effect on their achievement.

Globalisation and decline of traditional 'men's jobs' Since the 1980s, globalisation has led to much manufacturing industry relocating to developing countries, leading to a decline in heavy industries like shipbuilding, mining, and manufacturing in the UK. Some argue that the resulting decline in male employment opportunities has led to a male 'identity crisis', with a loss of motivation and self-esteem. Many boys now believe they have little prospect of getting jobs and so cease trying to get qualifications.

Feminisation of schooling Sewell (2006) argues that boys fall behind because education has become 'feminised'. Schools no longer nurture 'masculine' traits, e.g. competitiveness and leadership.

▶ Some argue that assessment has been feminised by the introduction of coursework and this disadvantages boys.

▶ Lack of male primary school teachers: only 1 in 6 primary school teachers are men and over 60% of 8-11 year old boys have no lessons with a male teacher. This may give boys the idea that education is a feminine activity.

Lack of male role models at home The increase in the number of female-headed lone parent families (around 1.5 million) means that now many boys grow up lacking a positive male role model who goes out to work to support a family. These boys may thus be less likely to see the value of employment and therefore also of qualifications.

'Laddish' subcultures may lead to boys' under-achievement. Studies show that there is peer pressure on boys to demonstrate their masculinity by being anti-school:

▶ **Francis** (2001) found that boys were more concerned than girls about being labelled by peers as swots, because this threatens their masculine identity. Working-class culture sees non-manual work (including schoolwork) as effeminate and inferior.

▶ **Epstein** (1998) found that pro-school working-class boys were likely to be harassed, labelled as 'gay' and subjected to verbal abuse.

Evaluation
Girls are now achieving more, but radical feminists argue that the education system remains patriarchal, e.g. sexual harassment of girls continues at school; education limits their subject choices and careers; secondary school heads are still more likely to be men.

Evaluation
Traditional male manual jobs needed few qualifications, so it seems unlikely that the disappearance of these jobs would affect boys' motivation to obtain qualifications.

Interpretation
Are 'laddish' subcultures an 'internal' or 'external' factor? You can make the point that they operate both inside and outside the school.

As girls move into traditional masculine areas such as paid work, boys become more 'laddish' in an effort to identify themselves as non-feminine and this leads to under-achievement.

Policies to raise boys' achievement

Concern about boys' under-achievement relative to girls has led to the introduction of a range of policies.

These often use boys' leisure interests (e.g. sport) and famous male role models and are aimed at improving boys' literacy skills and motivation to achieve. Examples include the *Raising Boys Achievement* project, the *Reading Champions* scheme and *Playing for Success*.

Gender and subject choice

Although girls have overtaken boys in achievement, there continue to be major gender differences in subject choice. Girls and boys follow different 'gender routes' in their subject choices.

▷ **In the National Curriculum**, most subjects are compulsory, but where choice is possible, girls and boys choose differently; e.g. in design and technology, girls choose food technology, boys choose resistant materials.

▷ **In post-16 education**, there is more choice available and big gender differences emerge; e.g. boys opt for maths and physics while girls choose modern languages, English and sociology. This pattern continues into higher education.

▷ **In vocational subjects**, gender segregation is at its greatest; only 1% of construction apprentices are female.

Explaining gender differences in subject choice

Several factors are responsible for gender differences in subject choice.

▷ **Early socialisation**

▷ **Gendered subject images**

▷ **Peer pressure**

▷ **Gendered career opportunities**

Early socialisation Gender role socialisation involves learning the behaviour expected of males and females.

▷ **In the family**, from an early age, boys and girls are dressed differently and given different toys, while boys are rewarded for being active and girls for being passive.

▷ **At school**, Byrne (1979) found, teachers encourage boys to be tough and show initiative, while they expect girls to be quiet, helpful, clean and tidy.

▷ **Leisure reading and subject choice** Murphy and Elwood (1998) found that boys read hobby books and information texts and so prefer science subjects, while girls read stories about people and prefer English.

Gender domains are tasks and activities seen as either male or female 'territory'; e.g. looking after an elderly person is 'female'. These views are shaped by children's early experiences and by the expectations of adults. Browne and Ross (1991) found that, when set open-ended tasks such as designing a boat, boys designed powerboats and battleships, while girls designed cruise ships, reflecting different gender domains. This affects subject choice: people's feelings are part of the female gender domain, so girls choose humanities; how things work is in the male domain, so boys choose science.

Gendered subject images Related to gender domains, subjects have a 'gender image' – they are seen as either male or female. For example, science is mainly taught by men and textbooks traditionally use boys' interests as examples. As a result, it is seen as a masculine subject, part of the male gender domain, and so is taken mostly by boys.

Peer pressure Other boys and girls pressurise individuals to conform. Boys often opt out of music because of negative peer response, while girls who choose sport have to contend with accusations from boys of being 'butch' or 'lesbian'. This also links to subject image and gender domains – sport is seen as masculine, music as feminine.

Gendered careers Many jobs are seen as either 'men's' or 'women's' and tend to be dominated by one gender – e.g. nursing and construction work. Vocational courses, which prepare young people for specific careers, therefore also tend to be dominated by one gender or the other.

Evaluation
Pupils in single-sex schools make less traditional subject choices. This may be because there is no opposite-sex peer pressure to conform to gender-stereotypical subject choices.

Gender identity and schooling

Pupils' school experiences may reinforce their gender and sexual identities.

▶ **Connell** (1995) argues that school reproduces 'hegemonic masculinity' – the dominance of heterosexual masculine identity and subordination of female and gay identities.

▶ **Feminists** argue that experiences in school act as a form of social control to reproduce patriarchy – male domination and female subordination. This happens in several ways:

Verbal abuse Name-calling puts girls down if they behave in certain ways and acts as a form of social control to make them conform to male expectations.

Analysis
These labels often do not reflect actual behaviour; they reinforce gender norms – e.g. boys may be called 'gay' simply for having female friends.

▶ **Lees** (1986) notes that boys call girls 'slags' if they appear sexually available, but there is no equivalent term for males. Paetcher notes that pupils police one another's sexual identities through negative labels.

▶ **Mac an Ghaill** (1992) found that anti-school working-class boys' subcultures use verbal abuse to reinforce their definitions of masculinity. They called other working-class boys who worked hard, 'dickhead achievers'.

Teachers Haywood and Mac an Ghaill (1996) found that male teachers reinforced gender identities by telling boys off for 'behaving like girls' and ignoring boys' verbal abuse of girls.

The male gaze is a form of social control where male pupils and teachers look girls up and down as sexual objects. Boys who don't participate may be labelled 'gay' – also a form of social control.

Double standards exist when one set of moral standards is applied to one group but a different set to another group. For example, Lees (1993) found that boys boast about their own sexual exploits, but label girls' negatively for the same behaviour.

ONE TO TRY

Question Outline some of the school factors that may lead to the educational under-achievement of boys. (12 marks)

Examiner's Advice There are 8 marks for your knowledge of these factors but also 4 marks for explaining or assessing them. Keep the focus of your answer on school factors such as lack of male teacher role models, male pupil anti-school subcultures, the 'feminisation' of education, emphasis on coursework etc. To get into the higher mark ranges you need to explain why each of these factors may lead to the under-achievement of boys, e.g. 'laddish' subcultures pressurise boys to conform to anti-school values that denigrate schoolwork and acceptance of authority. You should only refer to non-school factors as a way of assessing the importance of school factors.

4 The Role of Education (1) Functionalism and the New Right

Key Issues
▶ What are functionalism and the New Right?
▶ What functions do functionalists see education as performing?
▶ What is the New Right view of the role of the market in education?
▶ What criticisms have been made of functionalist and New Right views of education?

Application
A very effective way to start an answer on the role of education is to outline the main assumptions of the theory under consideration.

The functionalist perspective on education

Functionalism is a consensus view that sees society as being essentially harmonious. It argues that:

▶ Society has basic needs, including the need for social order. To survive, society needs social solidarity through everyone sharing the same norms and values. Otherwise, society would disintegrate.

▶ Social institutions such as education perform positive functions both for society as a whole and for individuals, by socialising new members of society and by helping to create and sustain social solidarity.

▶ Functionalism is a conservative view of society.

The main contributors to the functionalist perspective on the role of education are Durkheim, Parsons, and Davis and Moore.

Durkheim: solidarity and skills

According to Durkheim (1903), education performs two basic functions:

Analysis
Whenever you use an important concept for the first time (such as social solidarity or the specialised division of labour), always explain what it means.

▶ **It promotes social solidarity** without which society would fall apart. By transmitting society's shared culture (its norms and values), education binds people together and enables them to cooperate. Teaching a common history and shared rituals (such as singing the national anthem) is important to show pupils they share the same past and have a common purpose. Education also teaches children to follow universalistic rules which are essential for cooperation in society.

▶ **Education prepares young people for work**. Industrial societies have a specialised division of labour which requires people to undergo often long periods of training for specific occupations. Education equips individuals with the specialist skills needed to participate in work in a modern economy.

Parsons: socialisation and meritocracy

Talcott Parsons (1961) argues that the school is the 'focal socialising agency' of modern society.

Analysis
Education performs both economic and social functions. It's useful to categorise them in this way in your answer.

Secondary socialisation During primary socialisation within the family, each child is treated differently – as someone who is 'special'. Wider society cannot function in this way – everyone has to be treated in the same way (e.g. all are equal before the law). Education teaches these universalistic standards and acts as a bridge between family and wider society. In particular, it socialises individuals into the shared values of a meritocratic society.

Meritocracy A meritocratic society is based upon two key values:

▶ **Individual achievement** Everyone achieves their status through their own efforts and abilities. It is not where you come from but what you can do that gives you your position in society.

▶ **Equal opportunity** for every individual to achieve their full potential.

Society in miniature School is a miniature version of wider society – both are meritocratic. In school, individuals succeed or fail depending on their own ability and effort. This prepares them for life in modern society and its economy, which is competitive and individualistic.

Davis and Moore: role allocation

For Davis and Moore (1945), the main function of education is role allocation – the selection and allocation of individuals to their future work roles. They present a functionalist explanation of social stratification as follows:

Application
Apply evidence on class, gender or ethnic inequalities to challenge Davis and Moore's arguments – e.g. 'Class differences in achievement suggest that not everyone actually has the same chance in education'.

▶ Some people are more talented than others.

▶ Some work roles are more complex than others and require greater skill.

▶ For society to function efficiently, the most talented individuals need to be allocated to most important jobs.

▶ Higher rewards are offered for these jobs to motivate everyone to strive for them.

▶ A meritocratic education system allows everyone to compete equally. It 'sifts and sorts' individuals so that the most talented get the best qualifications and are allocated to the most important jobs.

▶ As a result, society is more productive because the most able people do the most important jobs.

Interpretation
Questions often ask about the 'main' function of education. If so, focus on the function suggested by the question (e.g. promoting solidarity) and use your knowledge of other functions to evaluate which one is the most important function.

Human capital theory This is a similar idea to Davis and Moore's view. Modern industrial society is technologically advanced, so the skills of its workforce are its main economic asset or 'capital'. A meritocratic education system is the best way to develop a sufficiently skilled workforce and thus create greater economic efficiency and higher living standards.

Evaluation of functionalism

▶ Marxists argue that the values transmitted by education are not society's shared values, but rather those of the ruling class.

▶ Education is not meritocratic, because schools discriminate against some groups (e.g. working-class and black pupils) and don't give them an equal opportunity to achieve.

Evaluation
Most evaluation is presented through criticisms, but it's good to emphasise a theory's strengths too – e.g. 'It is difficult to argue against the need for social solidarity to keep a society of tens of millions of people together'.

▶ Hargreaves (1982) argues that schools place more value on competition and developing individuals than on developing a sense of social solidarity, as Durkheim claims.

▶ It is sometimes difficult to see a direct link between the subjects studied at school and what is required of workers in their jobs. Education doesn't necessarily equip people for future work roles.

▶ Interactionists argue that the functionalist view of socialisation is too deterministic. Not all pupils passively accept the school's values – some reject and rebel against them.

▶ A person's ascribed characteristics – their class background, gender and ethnicity – are more important in determining their income later in life than is their achievement in school.

The New Right perspective on education

The New Right is more of a political than a sociological perspective. However, the New Right is of interest to sociologists because:

▶ It is a more recent conservative view than functionalism.

▶ It has influenced educational policy in Britain and elsewhere.

Functionalism and the New Right compared

New Right ideas are similar to those of functionalism:

▶ They believe that some people are naturally more talented than others.

▶ They agree with functionalists that education should be run on meritocratic principles of open competition.

▶ They believe that education should socialise pupils into shared values and provide a sense of national identity.

In addition, the New Right believe that older industrial societies such as Britain are in decline, partly as a result of increased global economic competition.

The market versus the state

The effects of state control A key feature of New Right thinking (not found in functionalism) is that too much state control of education (as well as other areas of social and economic life) has resulted in inefficiency, national economic decline and a lack of personal and business initiative. A culture of state welfare dependency has developed, the cost of which has reduced investment in industry.

One size fits all New Right arguments are based on the belief that the state cannot meet people's needs. In a state-run education system, education inevitably ends up as 'one size fits all' that does not meet individual and community needs, or the needs of employers for skilled and motivated workers.

Lower standards State-run schools are not accountable to those who use them – pupils, parents and employers – and so they are inefficient. Schools that get poor results do not change because they are not answerable to their consumers. The result is lower standards and a less qualified workforce.

The solution: marketisation

For the New Right, the issue is how to make schools more responsive to their 'consumers'. In their view, the solution is the marketisation of education. Marketisation is the introduction into areas run by the state (such as education or the NHS) of market forces of consumer choice and competition between suppliers (such as schools or hospitals).

The New Right argue that creating an 'education market' forces schools to respond to the needs of pupils, parents and employers. For example, competition with other schools means that teachers have to be more efficient. A school's survival depends on its ability to raise the achievement levels of its pupils.

Chubb and Moe: giving the consumer choice

▶ Chubb and Moe (1990) compared the achievements of 60,000 pupils from low-income families in 1,015 state and private high schools in the USA.

▶ The data shows that pupils from low-income families do about 5% better in private schools. This suggests that state education is not meritocratic.

▶ State education has failed to create equal opportunity because it does not have to respond to pupils' needs.

Application
When dealing with a question on functionalist views of education's role, bring in the New Right too – their arguments are in some ways an extension of the functionalists'.

Evaluation
One major difference with functionalism is that the New Right doesn't believe the state can run an efficient education system.

Application
Link New Right ideas to examples of marketisation policies (see Topic 6). Explain how these reflect New Right thinking – e.g. 'Formula funding means schools have an incentive to be successful, since those that attract more pupils get more money'.

Analysis
Explain how vouchers might raise standards – e.g. 'Vouchers would be schools' main source of income. Schools would have to compete to attract parents' vouchers by improving the quality of education they offer. Those that did so would grow, while schools that did not, would close'.

▷ Parents and communities cannot do anything about failing schools while the schools are controlled by the state.

▷ Private schools deliver higher quality education because they are answerable to paying consumers – the parents.

The solution Chubb and Moe's answer to the supposed inefficiency of state schools is to introduce a market system in state education – that is, give control to consumers (parents and local communities). This should be done via a voucher system in which each family would be given a voucher to spend on buying education from a school of their choice.

Has the state any role in education?

Although the New Right want to reduce the state's role in education, they do still see a limited role for it:

▷ The state should create the framework for competition between schools (e.g. by publishing league tables of exam results and by setting a national curriculum that all schools must teach).

▷ The state still has to ensure that schools transmit society's shared culture through a curriculum that emphasises a shared national identity (e.g. through the teaching of British history).

Evaluation of the New Right

Evaluation
The New Right view rests on their claim that state control is the cause of education's problems. If other factors are the real cause, the New Right argument falls apart.

▷ Although school standards – as measured by exam results – seem to have risen, there are other possible reasons for this improvement apart from the introduction of a market.

▷ Critics argue that low standards in some state schools are the result of inadequate funding rather than state control of education.

▷ Gewirtz argues that competition between schools benefits the middle class, who can get their children into more desirable schools.

▷ Marxists argue that education imposes the culture of a ruling class, not a shared culture or 'national identity' as the New Right argue.

ONE TO TRY

Read Item A and answer the question that follows.

Item A
Writing from a functionalist perspective, Parsons argues that education performs certain key functions. Education socialises young people into society's shared values such as an emphasis on individual achievement and meritocratic values. Schools are miniature versions of society in which individuals succeed or fail according to their own ability and effort. This prepares children for life in modern society in which work is competitive and individualistic.

By contrast, Marxists argue that the values transmitted by education are not society's shared values but those of the ruling class.

Question Using material from **Item A** and elsewhere, assess functionalist views of the role of education in modern society.   (20 marks)

Examiner's Advice You should identify and explain the functions that functionalists such as Parsons, Durkheim and Davis and Moore see education performing. Link their views to the central functionalist claim that there is a value consensus in society. Use key ideas such as meritocracy, role allocation and education acting as a bridge between family and society. You could draw on the arguments of New Right thinkers to support functionalist claims. Assess functionalist views by offering some criticisms of them, especially from a Marxist perspective. You could also put forward criticisms from feminist and interactionist sociologists.

5 The Role of Education (2) Marxism

Key Issues
▶ What are the main features of the Marxist view of society?
▶ What do Marxists see as the role of education in modern society?
▶ What criticisms have been made of Marxist views?

What is Marxism?

Marxism is a conflict view that sees society as being based on class divisions and exploitation. Marxists argue that:

▶ In capitalist society there are two classes – the ruling class (capitalists, or bourgeoisie) and the subject class (working class, or proletariat).

▶ The capitalist class own the means of production (land, factories etc) and make their profits by exploiting the labour of the working class.

▶ This creates class conflict that could threaten the stability of capitalism or even result in a revolution to overthrow it.

▶ Social institutions (such as the education system, the mass media, religion etc) reproduce class inequalities and play an ideological role by persuading exploited workers that inequality is justified and acceptable.

Analysis
When you present your account of Marxist views of education, begin by briefly explaining the basic assumptions Marxism makes about capitalist society.

Althusser: the ideological state apparatus

Despite the inequalities in the system, capitalists are able to hold on to power because they control the state. Althusser (1971) claims the state consists of two elements which help to keep them in power:

▶ **The repressive state apparatus** (RSA) When necessary to protect capitalist interests, the state uses force to repress the working class via the police, courts and army.

▶ **The ideological state apparatus** (ISA) controls people's ideas, values and beliefs. The ISA includes religion, the mass media and the education system.

The education system performs two functions as an ISA:

▶ **Reproduction** Education reproduces class inequality, by failing each generation of working-class pupils in turn and thereby ensuring that they end up in the same kinds of jobs as their parents.

▶ **Legitimation** Education legitimates (justifies) class inequality by producing ideologies (sets of ideas and beliefs) that disguise its true cause. Education tries to convince people that inequality is inevitable and that failure is the fault of the individual, not the capitalist system.

Analysis
Explain the difference between *reproducing* inequality (by failing working-class pupils) and *legitimating* or justifying inequality (convincing them of the fairness of capitalism). Reproduction affects pupils' life chances, while legitimation affects what they believe and how they respond to capitalism.

Bowles and Gintis

▶ According to Bowles and Gintis (1976), capitalism needs workers with the kind of obedient attitudes and submissive personality-type that is willing to accept hard work, low pay and authority.

▶ Like Althusser, they see the role of the education system in capitalist society as reproducing an obedient, exploitable workforce that will accept social inequality as inevitable and fair. To achieve this, successive generations of workers need these ideas firmly planted in their minds – and this is the function of the education system.

▶ Bowles and Gintis argue that there is a close correspondence (similarity or parallel) between relationships in school and those found in the workplace. This similarity creates new generations of workers ready to accept their lot and serve capitalism.

Analysis
Explain *why* an obedient workforce is so important to capitalism – what would happen if they were not obedient?

The correspondence principle

According to Bowles and Gintis, schooling takes place in 'the long shadow of work'. The relationships and structures found in education mirror or correspond to those of work.

In capitalist society, school is like work in many ways.

How school mirrors work

Application
Remember that you gain marks for using appropriate concepts such as alienation and fragmentation of knowledge – and for explaining what they mean.

School	Work
Alienation – pupils' lack control over education.	Alienation through workers' lack of control over production.
Hierarchy of authority: head > teachers > pupils (and sometimes prefects).	Hierarchy of authority: boss > supervisor > workers.
Extrinsic satisfaction (rewards) rather than from interest in the subjects studied.	Extrinsic rewards – pay, not satisfaction from the job itself.
Fragmentation of knowledge into unconnected subjects.	Fragmentation of work into small, meaningless tasks.
Competition and divisions among pupils.	Competition and divisions among workers – differences in status and pay.

The hidden curriculum

The correspondence principle operates through the hidden curriculum – all the 'lessons' that are learnt in school without being directly taught. Through the everyday workings of the school, pupils accept hierarchy, competition, alienation etc. It becomes simply the normal way to think.

The myth of meritocracy: legitimating class inequality

Interpretation
Be clear what Bowles and Gintis mean by a 'myth'. It's an idea that, although untrue, is designed to create a particular way of thinking – in this case, to justify inequality in education and capitalist society.

The education system helps to prevent people from recognising their exploited position and rebelling against the system, by legitimating class inequalities. It does this by producing ideologies (sets of ideas) that explain why inequality is fair, natural and/or inevitable.

The education system creates many myths, including the 'myth of meritocracy'. Functionalists argue that education and the world of work are both meritocratic, because in their view everyone has an equal opportunity to achieve. Those who gain the highest rewards deserve them because they are the most able and hardworking.

However, Bowles and Gintis argue that this is a myth. In reality, success is based on class background, not ability or educational achievement. But by promoting the (untrue) claim that rewards are based on ability, the myth of meritocracy helps persuade workers to accept inequality and their subordinate position as legitimate.

Role allocation

Bowles and Gintis reject the functionalist claim that education allocates the most talented people meritocratically to the most important and best-rewarded roles. Their research found that it was obedient students who got the best grades, not those who were non-conformist or creative thinkers. That is, the education system rewards those who conform to the qualities required of the future workforce.

> **Evaluation**
> Remember that you can use Bowles and Gintis' arguments in an answer to a question on functionalism, because they are an important critique of functionalist claims that education is meritocratic.

Willis: learning to labour

Using qualitative methods, Willis (1977) studied the counter-school culture of 'the lads' – a group of 12 working-class boys – as they made the transition from school to work.

Willis rejects Bowles and Gintis's version of the correspondence principle. Rather than the lads passively accepting ruling-class ideology (such as the myth of meritocracy), he found that working-class pupils may resist attempts to indoctrinate them in school. They are able to partially see through the meritocratic ideology that claims working-class pupils can get on through hard work.

> **Analysis**
> Although Willis is a Marxist, his view of how the education system reproduces inequality differs from Bowles and Gintis'. It's important to point out the differences among Marxists as well as those between Marxism and theories like functionalism.

The counter-school culture The lads formed a distinct counter-culture that was opposed to the school. They flouted the school's rules (e.g. by smoking, disrupting classes and playing truant). For the lads, such acts of defiance were ways of resisting the school's authority.

This anti-school counter-culture is similar to the shopfloor culture of male manual workers. The lads identify strongly with male manual work and this explains why they see themselves as superior both to girls and to the 'effeminate' ear'oles (conformist pupils) who aspire to non-manual jobs.

For Willis, the irony is that by resisting the school's ideology, the lads' counter-school culture guarantees that they will fail, thereby ensuring that they end up in the manual work that capitalism needs someone to perform. Thus, their resistance to school ends up reproducing class inequality.

> **Evaluation**
> Rather than leaving all your evaluative points until the end, it's more effective to make them throughout your answer. As you explain part of the theory, add a critical point – so you pick up evaluation marks throughout.

Business and education

Some Marxists have claimed that recent educational policies in the UK make their analysis of the role of education even more relevant today.

▶ Marketisation policies, the privatisation of some educational services, business sponsorship of state schools (e.g. academies) etc result in more direct capitalist control over education and training.

▶ Not only does the education system function to provide a willing workforce for capitalism, but increasingly it does so while making profits for capitalists.

Evaluation – how useful is the Marxist view of education?

Marxists have exposed the 'myth of meritocracy' and shown how education can serve the interests of capitalism by reproducing and legitimating class inequalities. However, sociologists from other perspectives are critical of the Marxist view:

Postmodernists argue that Marxism is out of date. The correspondence principle no longer operates or is at the very least too simplistic a view.

▶ Postmodernists argue that class divisions are no longer important in a post-Fordist economic system that is now much more diverse and fragmented.

▶ They claim that where Marxists see inequality, there is really diversity and choice.

Feminists argue that schools reproduce not only capitalism, but patriarchy too. McRobbie points out that females are largely absent from Willis' study. However, Willis' study has been the model for research into other educational inequalities, including gender, ethnicity and sexuality.

Marxists disagree among themselves as to how reproduction and legitimation take place. Bowles and Gintis take a deterministic view and assume that pupils passively accept indoctrination. Willis rejects this simple 'brainwashing' view and shows how pupils may resist school and yet still end up in working-class jobs.

Romanticisation Willis has been criticised for romanticising the 'lads', presenting them as working-class heroes despite their anti-social behaviour and sexist attitudes. His study of only 12 boys in one school is also unlikely to be representative.

Evaluation

Evaluation isn't just about criticisms. Discuss strengths too – e.g. 'Although Marxists have been criticised, they do highlight how education maintains class inequality'.

ONE TO TRY

Read Item A and answer the question that follows.

Item A
Marxism is a conflict view that sees society as based on class divisions and exploitation. Education functions in the interests of the ruling class in a number of ways. Althusser argues that education is an ideological state apparatus controlling people's ideas, values and beliefs.

In particular, education reproduces class inequality, failing each generation of working-class pupils in turn. It also legitimates class inequality by producing ideologies that disguise its true cause. Education tries to convince people that inequality is inevitable and that failure is the fault of the individual. Marxists argue that schooling takes place in 'the long shadow of work'.

Other sociologists such as functionalists and the New Right disagree with Marxist explanations. They argue that education performs positive functions for society as a whole.

Question Using material from **Item A** and elsewhere, assess Marxist explanations of the role of education in modern society.   (20 marks)

Examiner's Advice You should identify and explain the functions that Marxists such as Althusser, Bowles and Gintis, and Willis see education performing in capitalist society. Link their views to the central Marxist claim that there is class division and conflict in capitalist society. Use key ideas such as legitimation and reproduction of class inequality, the correspondence principle, the myth of meritocracy and the hidden curriculum in your answer. Assess Marxist views by offering some criticisms of them, especially from a functionalist perspective. You could also put forward criticisms from feminist and interactionist sociologists.

6 Educational Policy

Analysis
Two issues run through
questions on policy:
selection and inequality.
Focus on these as you
cover each policy – does
it reduce or increase
inequality and how does it
affect selection?

Key Issues

▶ How have educational policies affected selection of pupils by schools?
▶ How have marketisation policies affected education?
▶ How have policies dealt with educational inequalities?

What is educational policy?

Educational policies are government strategies for education, introduced through legal changes and instructions to schools. Until the 19th century, education was only provided by church or private schools. However, industrialisation created a need for an educated and trained workforce and this led to the development of compulsory state-run education.

The development of state education

State education in Britain has gone through several stages of development. Miriam David (1993) identifies these as:

Phase 1: 1870-1944 The middle class received an academic education for future professional careers, while the working class had elementary schooling in basic skills for factory work and left school early.

Phase 2: 1944-1988 Initially the **tripartite system** (introduced in 1944) used the 11+ exam to allocate pupils to secondary school. In practice, this channelled middle-class children into grammars and working-class pupils into non-academic education in secondary moderns.

Interpretation
Note that comprehensives
never covered the whole
of Britain – grammar
schools were retained in
some areas.

From 1965, the **comprehensive system** was introduced in most parts of Britain, replacing grammar and secondary modern schools with comprehensive schools that all pupils in an area attended. However, inequalities were still reproduced because most schools streamed their pupils – working-class children were disproportionately placed in lower streams.

Phase 3: since 1988 The Conservative government introduced the Education Reform Act (ERA) in 1988. It had **marketisation** at its core. After 1997 New Labour policies continued to maintain an education market.

Marketisation policies

Analysis
Show analysis by
explaining how each policy
creates a market – e.g.
'Publishing schools' exam
results means parents can
make an informed choice
about where to send
their children'.

Policies since 1988 have developed an education market, reducing state control and introducing parental choice and competition between schools. This was based on New Right arguments that competition forces schools to improve in order to attract 'customers' (i.e. parents) and therefore raises standards. David calls this a **parentocracy**. Examples of marketisation policies include: exam leagues tables; publication of Ofsted inspection reports; open enrolment; formula funding; business sponsorship, and specialist schools.

Marketisation, inequality and selection

Ball and Whitty claim that marketisation reproduces inequality because publication of league tables means schools with good results are more in demand with parents, so these schools can be more selective. This means they can select high-achieving pupils – who are more likely to be middle-class (and female).

Application
Link marketisation to
inequality and selection –
e.g. 'Because middle-class
parents know how the
education system works,
they can give their children
a better chance of getting
into a good school'.

Because schools are funded according to the numbers they attract, popular schools with good results get more money and can afford more teachers and other resources. In turn, this means they attract even more high-achieving pupils, leading to even better results. The process works in reverse for schools with poor results. Middle-class pupils benefit most from this process.

Ball argues that marketisation also **legitimates** inequality. The idea of 'parent power' (parentocracy) gives the image of parents being in control and able to choose their child's school – so any differences in achievement are seen as the parents' fault for choosing badly, not the system's fault for being unfair. Gewirtz et al argue that in reality, middle-class parents have more economic and cultural capital and thus more choice, e.g. they can move into the catchment area of a better school.

New Labour policies

Under New Labour governments after 1997, spending on education increased substantially. The two aims of New Labour's policies from 1997 onwards were:

▶ **Promoting diversity and choice** by maintaining the education market. Policies include competition between schools, creating Specialist Schools and setting up Academies.

▶ **Reducing inequality of opportunity** in education. Policies include Educational Maintenance Allowances (EMAs), Education Action Zones (EAZs) and Aim Higher.

Evaluation of New Labour policies

▶ The policies are contradictory, e.g. EMAs help poorer pupils stay on post-16, but they now have to pay university tuition fees.

▶ New Labour has left the private education system untouched.

▶ 'Choice' and 'diversity' are just nice ways of saying 'inequality' – the education market ensures working-class pupils remain disadvantaged.

▶ On the other hand, more education spending and a focus on a 'learning society' have been genuine achievements. Evidence that academies have raised standards is mixed – some show improved results, others don't.

Ethnicity and policy

Policies relating to ethnicity have gone through three stages. In the 1960s and 70s, the aim was to encourage **assimilation**, e.g. through English as a Second Language programmes. In the 1980s and 1990s, the aim switched to valuing all cultures through **multi-cultural education** policies such as black studies in the mainstream curriculum. More recently, the focus has been on **social inclusion**, e.g. the legal duty on schools to promote racial equality, but Mirza criticises even the more recent policies as being too limited in scope.

Gender and policy There have been a number of important policies aimed at reducing gender inequalities in achievement and at promoting non-traditional subject choices. See Topic 3 for details.

Evaluation
Point out the contradiction – how can competition work without producing inequality? All markets produce winners and losers.

Evaluation
Evaluate New Labour policies in terms of how far they have reduced inequalities and raised standards.

Interpretation
If a question is about 'social inequalities', you should discuss policies that address gender (see Topic 3) and ethnicity as well as class inequality.

ONE TO TRY

Question Outline some of the education policies that attempt to reduce inequalities in achievement. (12 marks)

Examiner's Advice There are 8 marks for your knowledge of these policies but also 4 marks for explaining or assessing them. Keep the focus of your answer on policies such as compensatory education, Sure Start, EMAs, multi-cultural and anti-racist education etc. To get into the higher mark ranges you need to explain why each policy may reduce educational inequalities, e.g. EMAs reduce some of the pressure on working-class pupils to earn money so as not to be a financial burden on their families. You could assess some of these policies by considering how effective they are in reducing inequalities in achievement.

Practice question and student answer

Read Item A and answer the question that follows.

Item A

Although it is difficult to define and measure the relationship between ethnicity and educational achievement, it is clear that pupils from some ethnic groups are not doing as well as pupils from other ethnic backgrounds. For example, pupils from Indian or Chinese backgrounds on average markedly outperform black and Pakistani pupils.

Some sociologists have put this down to the influence of factors outside the education system itself, such as family structure and expectations, material deprivation and racism. Some have even argued that pupils from some minority ethnic backgrounds are 'culturally deprived' and have poorer language skills and less motivation because of their family background.

However, others argue that it is what goes on in school that is most important because that is where education and learning takes place.

Question

Using material from **Item A** and elsewhere, assess the claim that ethnic differences in educational achievement are the result of factors outside the education system.   (20 marks)

Student Answer by Joe

> This is a good start that picks up on something in the Item and attaches an example to it.

It is important to start by recognising that ethnicity is difficult to define and measure. Everyone has an ethnicity but which should sociologists focus on? In the past the term 'Asian' was used, but this includes groups from a wide range of different ethnicities. Even so, pupils from some ethnic groups far outperform others, while white pupils' achievements are close to the national average.

> Joe shows a good knowledge of material on cultural deprivation and links it to the New Right perspective.

Sociologists have identified several factors outside the school that may explain why some ethnic groups do better than others. One such explanation is the cultural deprivation model. The argument here is that something in the home background culture causes problems with the pupil's education. New Right thinker Murray claims that a high proportion of black families are headed by lone mothers and the lack of the male role model in the home causes problems, particularly for boys. This is a failure of primary socialisation.

> Joe applies some relevant knowledge of cultural deprivation views here and in the previous paragraph.

Other cultural deprivation theories have examined the part played by language. Some sociologists have claimed that the language spoken by some minority ethnic pupils is ungrammatical and limited in other ways. This means they cannot explain things properly or understand everything done in schools. For some pupils, English is not their first language and isn't spoken in the home. This makes them less familiar with the language used in school.

> This is a well-developed criticism. Keddie's point is not just identified but it is explained as well – gaining marks for analysis.

However, some have strongly criticised the whole idea of cultural deprivation. Keddie calls it 'victim-blaming'. In other words, it is an example of finding something in the home culture that is different and developing an explanation for why this causes educational failure. How can a lone-parent family structure and an extended family structure both be a cause of under-achievement? Maybe there are just differences rather than deficiencies.

> It is good that Joe avoids slipping into a 'social class' answer, but this paragraph is a little underdeveloped and has no evaluation.

There is also the possibility that some minority ethnic groups suffer from material deprivation as well. Some – but not all – minority children come from working-class homes. They are more likely to live in poverty and this can have a bad effect on their education. There is a strong link between poverty and under-achievement since pupils from these backgrounds lack books, computers and the money to buy educational resources or to go on trips.

> This is a good summary of the 'other side of the coin'. It doesn't go on at such length that it turns the essay into an equally balanced 'school versus non-school factors' answer.

Some sociologists, especially from interactionist perspectives, have argued that it is not factors external to the school that cause ethnic differences in achievement, but what goes on in school itself. For example, Gillborn and Youdell claim that many teachers have 'racialised expectations' of pupils – in other words, they expect different behaviour and attitudes from different ethnic groups. Teachers expect black boys in particular to behave poorly and then they react strongly to any hint of such behaviour. As Sewell points out, this can feed into the creation of an anti-school subculture among some black boys. However, Fuller and Mac an Ghaill argue that this labelling process does not always result in failure because sometimes pupils reject these labels.

15/20

How to turn this into a top-mark answer

Joe's answer is a good response. Not much extra is needed to improve it to 16+/20. It already has some analysis (through explanation), some evaluation and some application (through examples). Crucially, he keeps a clear focus on non-school issues. However, there are several things that he could do to increase his mark and take the essay into the top mark band.

White pupils

This answer makes no mention at all of white pupils. It is a common error to equate ethnicity with non-white culture. It would have been stronger if he had examined some of the research that focuses on white – particularly working-class – pupils.

Linking school and non-school factors

One way to get into the top mark band is to see internal and external factors not as being completely separate things but as being linked together. For example, Joe could have argued that aspects of 'street culture' may be carried into the school in the form of anti-school subcultures. The peer group pressure involved in such subcultures does not start and end at the school gates.

Evaluation

The essay lacks a final evaluative conclusion – did Joe get his time management slightly wrong? You could conclude by noting that it is not always easy to separate the influence of factors outside school and those inside – e.g. racist ideas exist in wider society, outside school, and these ideas may influence how teachers perceive and treat pupils from minority ethnic groups.

CHAPTER 3 RESEARCH METHODS

1 Key Concepts and Choice of Method

Key Issues
▶ How do positivist and interpretivist approaches to research differ?
▶ What key concepts are used to judge the usefulness of research methods?
▶ What factors affect the sociologist's choice of research method and research topic?

Positivism versus interpretivism

Positivists argue that there is a measurable, objective social reality that exists 'out there', just like the physical world. They see our behaviour as the result of social forces shaping what we do, and the aim of research is to discover the underlying causes of our behaviour.

They use standardised methods of research, such as questionnaires, structured interviews, structured observation and official statistics. This enables them to obtain reliable and representative quantitative data. They use this data to identify general patterns and trends in behaviour, from which they produce cause-and-effect explanations like those in the natural sciences.

Interpretivists claim that there is no objective social reality, just the subjective meanings that social actors give to events. Therefore, the aim of research is to uncover actors' meanings or worldview.

For interpretivists, this means using open-ended research methods that produce valid, qualitative data, such as unstructured interviews, participant observation and personal documents. Such methods enable the sociologist to gain understanding by experiencing the group's lifestyle for themselves, or by allowing individuals to explain their worldview in their own words, without the sociologist imposing their own views on the research subjects.

Three key concepts

Sociologists use three key concepts to judge the usefulness of a research method. These are:
▶ **Reliability**
▶ **Representativeness**
▶ **Validity**

Reliability

For a method to be reliable, it must be replicable, i.e. exactly repeatable to obtain the same results, regardless of who actually carries out the research. Reliability also means using standardised forms of measurement. A reliable method creates data that can be used to systematically re-test hypotheses about social behaviour.

Evaluation
The relationship between sociological theory and research methods is very important. The sociologist's position affects their choice of research method, the kind of questions asked, the type of data collected, and whether the reliability and representativeness of data, or its validity, is seen as more important.

Analysis
With a question on a particular method, start your answer by explaining why either positivists or intrepretivists prefer to use that method – and why the other approach doesn't.

Analysis
You must apply these three concepts to every research method. They are the essential 'vocabulary' to use in answer to any question about methods. Explain what it is about structured methods that produces reliable data and what it is about unstructured methods that produces valid data.

Positivists favour a scientific approach emphasising the need for reliability and therefore they use structured research methods that can be repeated, such as experiments, questionnaires and structured interviews. Positivists regards participant observation and unstructured interviews as unreliable because they cannot be repeated and do not use a standardised system of measurement.

Representativeness

Analysis
Make sure you can explain how a sample can be representative and why this allows generalisations to be made.

Sociologists cannot usually study every member of the group they are interested in because generally there are simply too many of them. Therefore researchers may choose to study only a sample – a smaller sub-group drawn from the wider target group.

To be representative, the characteristics of the sample need to be the same as those of the wider group. This allows the researcher to be more confident that what is true for the sample is probably also true for the whole group. This means they will be able to make generalisations (statements about the wider group) on the basis of evidence from the sample.

Analysis
Validity versus reliability: validity involves getting to a true account of people's meanings. Reliability involves measuring things in a standardised way that others can repeat. It is unlikely that a person's subjective meanings can be satisfactorily measured in an objective, standardised way. Methods that are strong on validity are usually weak on reliability and vice versa.

Positivists emphasise the importance of representativeness, because they wish to discover general patterns and make general cause-and-effect statements about social behaviour.

Validity

Validity refers to how authentic and true the data is. The aim of any research is to 'get close to the reality' of a social situation. Interpretivists emphasise the need to use methods such as participant observation or unstructured interviews which reveal the meanings people hold. Surveys, experiments and other structured research techniques are rejected because they do not reveal what social actors really think or how they act.

Primary and secondary data

Primary data is evidence collected by sociologists themselves for their own sociological purposes. This is material collected firsthand by researchers using methods such as questionnaires, observation and interviews.

Secondary data is any information that has already been collected by someone else for their own purposes and that may then be used by the sociologist. Official statistics, business records, media reports, diaries and personal documents are common forms of secondary data – as are the findings from existing sociological research that a later sociologist may go on to use.

Evaluation
Right at the start of an answer on choice of method, point out that methodological issues are the first consideration. Practical and ethical issues then tend to limit the sociologist's choice.

Choice of research method

Three main factors influence the sociologist's choice of research method:

▶ **the methodological preference of the sociologist**

▶ **practical aspects of research**

▶ **ethical concerns**

Methodological preference

Analysis
Explain why being a positivist or an interpretivist leads to a preference for particular methods, e.g. 'Positivists prefer official statistics because they are standardised and comparable year-on-year, so they generate quantitative data for the positivist to see patterns in behaviour'.

Positivists prefer quantitative data. In their view, the aim of research is to reveal cause-and-effect relationships. This requires quantitative data to identify patterns and trends in behaviour. Positivists thus prefer to use structured research techniques, e.g. questionnaires, which generate reliable, representative data.

Interpretivists prefer qualitative data. In their view, the aim of research is to uncover the meanings people hold. The only way to do this is to allow them to act or speak in the ways they feel are appropriate. This is best achieved by unstructured research methods such as participant observation and unstructured interviews, which produce valid, qualitative data. (See the start of this Topic for further explanation of positivism and interpretivism.)

Practical factors

Practical factors restrict the sociologist's choice of method. These include:

Time Some methods usually take more time, e.g. participant observation studies and unstructured interviews take more time than social surveys.

Finance The finance available affects the number of researchers, respondents and the amount of research time. Some methods are cheaper than others, e.g. postal questionnaires are cheap because researchers do not have to spend long periods of time talking to respondents or observing their behaviour.

Source of funding Research sponsored by government, businesses, voluntary organisations etc. reflects the concerns of these funding bodies. It is often easier to get funding for quantitative research.

Personal factors Researchers have careers, family commitments etc, so they may not be able to do lengthy research in the field.

Research subjects Some groups are less open, e.g. criminals, so structured research methods are not appropriate.

Research opportunity If a research opportunity suddenly appears, the researcher may have no time to prepare lengthy questionnaires or interview schedules.

Personal danger Methods involving direct contact with a research group increase the possibility of danger to researchers.

Ethical factors

Sociological research does not take place in a moral vacuum; sociologists have to think about the possible effects their research might have on people's lives.

Consent Researchers should have the informed consent of research subjects because of the effects that the research may have on them. People should not be manipulated or misled about the research.

Confidentiality Research subjects have a right to anonymity, so they should not be identifiable when research is published. This is difficult to achieve with small groups – even changing names may not be enough for anonymity.

Effects on research subjects Research findings can be used by political groups or the media in ways that may damage the research subjects.

Evaluation: which factor is most important?

Theoretical factors are a *positive influence* because they are about the kind of data the sociologist prefers to have – quantitative or qualitative. Practical and ethical factors are more of a limitation on choice of method.

Practical, ethical and theoretical concerns are often interrelated. For example, collecting qualitative data produces practical problems such as gaining trust, access etc, while gathering quantitative data creates practical problems such as sampling frames, the geographical distribution of a sample, question design etc.

Triangulation Some sociologists see advantages in both types of data. Triangulation combines quantitative and qualitative methods so that the strengths of one balance the weaknesses of the other.

Application
Referring to examples of research gains marks but be careful not to go into long descriptions of a study – keep it short and attached to the point you're making, such as: 'for example, Pryce spent months at a time in the field during his PO study of black communities in Bristol'.

Analysis
Be clear in sorting out which issues are practical, ethical or theoretical. Point out some that cross over more than one category, e.g. placing others in danger is both a practical and an ethical issue.

Analysis
Different methods have different ethical problems. Experiments have more problems with consent whilst unstructured interviews may have problems of confidentiality because of the high degree of trust involved.

Interpretation
Although questions are often about choice of *method*, occasionally they may be on choice of *topic* – so take particular care in reading questions like these.

Choice of topic

The sociologist's choice of topic is affected by several factors, including:

Practical factors Some topics may not easily be studied, e.g. high-level political decision-making may be inaccessible to the sociologist.

Funding bodies These have enormous influence because they will only fund studies of topics that they consider to be important. Governments are much more likely to fund research that links to their policies.

Society's values change and the interest in particular topics and issues moves with them.

The sociologist's theoretical perspective may affect whether or not they will become involved in studying a particular topic – e.g. feminists are likely to study gender issues.

Chance Sometimes, sociologists find themselves in a potential research situation by pure chance – e.g. hospitalisation as a result of illness gave one researcher the opportunity to do a study of a hospital ward.

ONE TO TRY

Question Examine the reasons why positivists prefer quantitative data while interpretivists prefer qualitative data. (20 marks)

Examiner's Advice This essay question carries 10 marks for AO1 and 10 marks for AO2. You can begin by briefly defining quantitative and qualitative data and giving one or two examples of methods that produce each type of data. Explain the connections between quantitative data and the positivists' scientific approach, using issues such as correlation, hypothesis testing, generalisations and cause-and-effect statements or scientific laws. Relate these to the key concepts of reliability and representativeness, explaining why methods that produce quantititve data may also produce reliable and representative data. Likewise, explain the links between qualitative data and interpretivism's goal of understanding actors' subjective meanings, and link this to the key interpretivist concept of validity. You can score evaluation marks by pointing out that practical issues such as the preferences of funding bodies for quantitative data play a part, as do ethical considerations and the nature of the topic being studied.

2 Experiments

Key Issues

▶ Why are laboratory experiments so rarely used by sociologists?

▶ What are the strengths and weaknesses of field experiments?

What are experiments?

The experiment is the main method of the natural sciences. The key feature of an experiment is the high degree of control that the researcher has over the situation. In an experiment, the researcher identifies and controls all the variables (factors) that might affect the outcome of the situation being studied. By manipulating the variables and observing what happens, the researcher can discover cause-and-effect relationships.

There are two main types of experiment:

▶ **Laboratory experiments**

▶ **Field experiments**

A laboratory experiment gives the researcher more control over variables, but it is more artificial. Field experiments, which take place in 'real-world' situations, are more true to life, but researchers cannot control all the variables.

Interpretation
In the opening paragraph of your answer, distinguish clearly between the different types of experiment.

Laboratory experiments

Positivists argue that there is a measurable objective social reality 'out there'. They take a scientific approach using standardised methods of research to obtain quantitative data that allows them to produce generalisations and cause-and-effect statements. They regard experiments (especially laboratory experiments) as very reliable, because they can be repeated exactly, allowing previous findings to be checked. Experiments also meet the positivists' requirement that data should be quantitative and scientifically collected.

Interpretivists claim that experiments do not translate easily to the study of social behaviour and they produce data that is low in validity. Moreover, because of a number of problems with laboratory experiments as a method, even positivists rarely make use of them in sociological research.

Evaluation
Because humans have consciousness and attach meanings to situations, this makes them unlike the subject matter of the natural sciences and makes experiments an unsuitable method.

Problems with laboratory experiments

▶ **Artificiality** The laboratory is a highly artificial environment and it is doubtful whether the results of experiments can be transferred to the real social world. How people react in an artificially constructed laboratory tells us very little about the way they act in real life situations. This means that the results of laboratory experiments often lack validity.

▶ **Identifying and controlling variables** The laboratory experiment is only effective if all the variables that can influence the outcome can be identified and controlled. The complexity of social interactions with a large number of influences at work means that it is impossible to identify, let alone control, all variables.

Application
Avoid lengthy descriptions of particular studies that use experiments. Instead, connect any examples of experiments to the strengths or weaknesses that you identify.

Interpretation
'Examine' questions often ask about *either* strengths or weaknesses (usually the latter for experiments). Focus mainly on whichever aspect the question states. Don't give a 'strengths versus weaknesses' answer.

Analysis
Explain why a characteristic of experiments is a weakness by linking it to validity, reliability or representativeness – e.g. 'most experiments are small-scale, so it is very difficult for them to be representative of a wider population'.

Interpretation
Don't slip into discussing participant observation when you are examining field experiments. They are different – experiments involve control over the situation, whereas PO doesn't.

▶ **Ethical issues** Many experiments involve some kind of 'blind' to conceal the real aims of the research from the subjects, so as to avoid this knowledge influencing their actions. This means that the researcher cannot obtain their *informed* consent. Another ethical problem is the emotional and psychological effects some experiments may have on those involved.

▶ **The Hawthorne effect** (or experimental effect) Even if the subjects are misled as to the real purpose of an experiment, their knowledge that they are in an experiment is likely to affect their behaviour. This reduces the validity of the experiment.

▶ **Limited application** The laboratory is a small place, so only small-scale social interaction can be studied. This excludes many of the most important sociological issues, such as large-scale social change. It is also impossible to study past events, or events of long duration, using experiments.

Field experiments

Field experiments take place in the real social world, where the sociologist either creates a situation or adapts an existing real-life situation to their research purpose. Those involved are usually unaware that an experiment is taking place. The aim of field experiments is to obtain some element of control while avoiding the artificiality of the laboratory.

Advantages

▶ **Less artificiality** Field experiments are set in real-world situations.

▶ **Validity** Because people are unaware of the experimental situation and are in their usual social environment, they will act normally. Their reactions will be genuine and the data collected will be high in validity.

Disadvantages

▶ **Less control over variables** Field experiments do not meet the rigorous scientific criteria of the laboratory experiment because the sociologist cannot control all the variables in the situation.

▶ **Limited application** There are relatively few situations that can be adapted to become a field experiment. Testing the influence of one factor – the apparent influence of social class, discriminatory actions, teacher expectations etc – in a limited way is possible, but anything more complex is very problematic. Field experiments also tend only to measure what people do, not why they do it.

▶ **Ethical problems** They do not usually gain the informed consent of those involved, because to do so would 'give the game away'.

ONE TO TRY

Question Examine the weaknesses of the experimental method as applied to the study of social behaviour. (20 marks)

Examiner's Advice There are 10 AO1 and 10 AO2 marks for this essay question. The focus of your answer should be on the weaknesses of experiments. You can refer to the strengths of this method, but only to evaluate these weaknesses.

You should cover both laboratory and field experiments. You can organise the weaknesses into theoretical, practical and ethical issues. Explain how intepretivists criticise laboratory experiments for their lack of validity and artificial nature.

3 Surveys and Sampling

Key Issues

▶ How are surveys constructed and carried out?

▶ What is a sample and why do sociologists use samples?

▶ How important is it for a research sample to be representative?

Social surveys

Surveys ask people questions about their lives, attitudes, opinions or behaviour. They take two basic forms:

▶ **Self-completion written questionnaires**

▶ **Interviews.**

Questions used in surveys can be of two types:

Evaluation
A good way to start an answer about these methods is to explain why positivists prefer closed-ended questions and why intepretivists prefer open-ended ones.

▶ **Closed-ended** questions: respondents choose their answer from a limited range of answers decided in advance by the researcher. Answers are often pre-coded for ease of analysis later.

▶ **Open-ended** questions: respondents are free to give whatever answer they wish, in their own words, without any pre-selected choices.

Conducting a survey

Aims Most surveys either have a general aim or seek to test a specific hypothesis. An aim is a statement that identifies what a sociologist intends to study. Often the aim is simply to collect data on a particular topic, for example, people's leisure patterns.

Hypotheses Other surveys seek to test one or more hypotheses. A hypothesis is more specific than an aim. It is a possible explanation that can be tested by collecting evidence to prove it true or false, e.g. that educational achievement is affected by gender.

Operationalising concepts Before research can begin, the researcher needs to define their sociological concepts or ideas in ways that can be measured. This process of converting a concept into something measurable is called 'operationalisation'. For example, 'educational achievement' might be defined as having passed five GCSEs at grades A*-C. However, when different sociologists operationalise the same concept differently, it becomes harder to compare their findings.

Analysis
The processes involved in a survey illustrate the reasons why positivists believe the survey is a more scientific approach to research.

The pilot study The next stage is to produce a draft questionnaire or interview schedule (the list of interview questions) and to give this a trial run. This is called a pilot study and its aim is to iron out any problems, refine or clarify questions and their wording, give interviewers practice etc.

Sampling

It is often impractical to study all the members of the research population or 'target group' that we are interested in, e.g. because of its sheer size, lack of time, money or other resources. Therefore researchers may only be able to a study a sample of it. A sample is a smaller part of the whole research population that the sociologist selects for study.

Sampling frames To select a sample of the research population, the sociologist first finds or creates a sampling frame – a list of all the members of the research population from which the sample can be chosen. For example, the electoral register is a list of all those entitled to vote.

Samples and representativeness

▶ To be representative, a sample should have the same characteristics, in the same proportions, as the wider research population. It should be a cross-section of the whole group.

▶ If the sample is a representative cross-section, then what is true of the sample is likely to be true of the whole group.

▶ Representativeness is important to positivists because they want to make **generalisations** and discover general laws of social behaviour.

Are all samples representative?

▶ Small samples are less likely to be representative of large populations.

▶ Interpretivists are more interested in the meanings held by social actors. Because they are not trying to establish 'laws' of social behaviour that might apply to large social groups, they feel it is less important to use representative samples.

▶ If the researcher does not have a sampling frame that includes all members of the research population, they cannot create a representative sample.

Types of sample

Sociologists use several types of sampling:

Random sampling This is where every member of the sampling frame has an equal chance of being selected (e.g. names drawn out of a hat). This eliminates bias in sample selection. A large enough random sample should reflect the characteristics (e.g. gender, class etc.) of the whole research population. However, not all random samples are large enough to ensure this happens.

Systematic or quasi-random sampling Some sociologists introduce an element of structure into sampling by selecting every *n*th person in the sampling frame – e.g. every tenth name in the list. This can reduce the chance of a skewed (biased) sample being randomly selected.

Stratified sampling The researcher first stratifies (breaks down) the population by age, class, gender etc. The sample is then created in the same proportions, e.g. if 20% of the population are under 16, then 20% of the sample also have to be under 16.

Quota sampling The population is stratified as above, and then each interviewer is given a quota of say, twenty females, ten of whom are aged 60 or over etc, which they have to fill with respondents who fit these characteristics. The interviewer keeps at this task until their quota is filled.

Analysis
Always explain the connections you make, e.g. 'Positivists emphasise a sample's representativeness because they do not want to make statements just about their small research sample – they want to be able to make statements about the group/population as a whole'.

Application
Learn some examples of 'ready-made' sampling frames in case you are asked a short question about them. These include phone directories, electoral registers and the Postcode Address File

Evaluation
With some social groups, e.g. professional criminals, it may be difficult to generate a sample. Sociologists therefore sometimes use a *snowball sample*, where one member of the group puts them in touch with another member and so on. However, such samples are unlikely to be representative.

Question

ONE TO TRY

(a) Explain the difference between stratified and snowball samples. (4 marks)

(b) Identify **two** other types of sample used by sociologists. (4 marks)

(c) Explain why representativeness is important in sampling. (2 marks)

(d) Suggest **two** reasons why a sample may not be representative. (4 marks)

(e) Explain what is meant by operationalisation of concepts. (2 marks)

4 Questionnaires

Key Issues

▶ What are the main characteristics of questionnaires?

▶ Why do positivists prefer questionnaires?

▶ What are the strengths and weaknesses of questionnaires?

What are questionnaires?

Written or self-completed questionnaires are the most common form of social survey. They can be distributed to people at home and returned by post, emailed or collected on the spot, e.g. in a classroom. Questionnaires ask respondents to answer pre-set questions. Questions tend to be closed-ended, often with pre-coded answers.

Why do positivists use questionnaires?

Analysis
To achieve high marks, it's vital that you explain the link between positivism and questionnaires.

Positivists start from the assumption that there is a measurable, objective social reality 'out there'. They take a scientific approach, using standardised methods of research to obtain quantitative data. This allows them to produce generalisations and cause-and-effect statements.

Positivists prefer questionnaires because they deliver reliable data – e.g. by using the same set of questions, they can be repeated exactly, so that previous findings can be re-tested. Questionnaires generate quantitative data that can be used to test hypotheses and identify correlations between variables, e.g. between education and class. They can also be used on a large scale to produce representative data. However, interpretivists claim that the data produced by questionnaires is low in validity.

Advantages of questionnaires

Practical advantages

Interpretation
If the question is about mailed or postal questionnaires, you must have a strong focus on the 'mailed' dimension as well as on questionnaires in general.

Questionnaires are quick and cheap, since there is no need to train interviewers or observers – respondents simply complete and return the questionnaires themselves. They gather large quantities of data from large numbers of people, widely spread geographically (especially if the questionnaire is a postal one). Pre-coded, closed-ended questions make the data easy to quantify.

Reliability

Positivists see questionnaires as a reliable method of collecting data. Because a questionnaire has a set list of questions and restricted choice of possible answers, it is easily replicated. By asking the same questions, we can compare the results obtained by different groups of people. There is also no researcher present to influence the respondent's answers.

Hypothesis testing

Questionnaires are useful for testing hypotheses about cause-and-effect relationships between different variables. For example, parental attitudes to education can be correlated with class.

Detachment and objectivity

Questionnaires are often completed with little or no personal contact between researchers and respondents, and so they are a good way of maintaining detachment and objectivity. Unlike interviews or observation, there is no bias caused by the presence of a researcher.

Analysis
Explain why a particular type of sample can be representative or why positivists emphasise the need for representativeness (see Topic 3 on samples).

Representativeness

Because questionnaires can collect information from large numbers of people, they increase the chance of obtaining a representative sample. So the findings of questionnaires are more likely to allow us to make accurate generalisations.

Disadvantages of questionnaires

Practical problems

Questionnaires need to be brief since most respondents are unlikely to complete a long, time-consuming questionnaire. This limits the amount of information that can be gathered. Sometimes the researcher has to offer incentives, e.g. a prize draw, to persuade respondents to complete the questionnaire.

Response rate

Evaluation
Explain disadvantages and advantages in relation to key concepts such as reliability, representativeness and validity – e.g. 'A low response rate distorts the representativeness of the sample, making generalisations unsound'.

Very low response rates are a major problem, especially with postal questionnaires. Few of those who receive a questionnaire bother to complete and return it. Complex language or bad design reduce response rates. A low response rate means that those who return their questionnaires may be different from those who don't, so results are unrepresentative.

Busy people may fail to respond, whereas people with time on their hands may be more likely to return questionnaires. Researchers may increase the response rate by sending out follow-up questionnaires, collecting by hand or offering incentives. However, this adds to the cost and time.

Inflexibility

Questionnaires are very inflexible. Once the questionnaire has been finalised, the researcher cannot explore any new areas of interest that might emerge during the course of the research.

Detachment

Interpretivists argue that questionnaire data lacks validity. Questionnaires involve little or no contact between researcher and respondent. This means that questions and answers cannot be clarified or misunderstandings cleared up. There is also no way of knowing whether the respondent and researcher both interpret the questions and answers in the same way.

Lying, forgetting and 'right answerism'

Respondents may lie, forget, not know, not understand, or try to please or annoy the researcher. Some may give socially desirable answers they feel they ought to give, rather than tell the truth. When respondents give answers that are not full or honest, this undermines the validity of the data.

Evaluation
Remember to connect points like these to one or more of the key concepts – in this case, explain why these factors reduce validity.

Imposing the researcher's meanings

Questionnaires may impose the researcher's meanings rather than revealing those of the respondent. The researcher chooses which questions to ask and decides the response categories, while closed-ended questions limit the answers respondents can give.

> **Question** Examine the advantages of using questionnaires in sociological research.
> (20 marks)
>
> **ONE TO TRY**
>
> **Examiner's Advice** There are 10 AO1 and 10 AO2 marks for this question. The focus of your answer should be on the advantages of using questionnaires. You can refer to the weaknesses of this method but only to evaluate these reasons.
>
> You should also explain that questionnaires are preferred by positivists because the data created is reliable and representative. You can organise your account of the advantages of questionnaires into theoretical, practical and ethical issues.

5 Interviews

Key Issues
▶ What types of interview are used by sociologists?
▶ What are the strengths and weaknesses of different types of interview?

Types of interview
Sociological research employs two main types of interview. These are:

▶ **Structured interviews**

▶ **Unstructured interviews** (including group interviews)

Sociologists sometimes also use semi-structured interviews, combining elements of both.

Interpretation
If the question is about 'interviews', then cover all varieties of interview. If it is on one particular type, focus on that type.

Structured interviews

The structured interview (sometimes called the formal or questionnaire interview) involves the face-to-face or over-the-phone delivery of a questionnaire. Structured interviews use an interview schedule – a pre-set list of questions designed by the researcher and asked of all interviewees in the same way. Interviewees then choose from a limited list of possible answers. Structured interviews are usually relatively brief.

Why do positivists use structured interviews?

Analysis
It's vital that you explain the link between positivism and structured interviews to achieve high marks.

Positivists start from the assumption that there is a measurable objective social reality. They take a scientific approach using standardised methods such as structured interviews to obtain quantitative data. Structured interviews employ fixed lists of closed-ended questions, so answers can be classified, counted and quantified. This allows the researcher to identify patterns and produce generalisations and cause-and-effect statements.

Positivists also prefer structured interviews because they are reliable (easily replicated by other researchers) and can produce fairly large-scale, representative data. However, interpretivists reject their use because they see them as lacking validity.

Advantages of structured interviews

Interpretation
'Examine' questions often ask about *either* strengths *or* weaknesses. Focus on whichever the question states. Don't give a 'strengths versus weaknesses' answer.

Reliability Because they use a fixed list of questions, with pre-coded response categories, structured interviews produce easily quantifiable data. As every interviewee's response is measured in the same way, structured interviews are a form of standardised measuring instrument. This means that the data from the different interviews is directly comparable.

Using the same fixed list of questions and possible answers also means that the structured interview is replicable and can be used to verify the results of earlier interviews or to identify changes over time.

Analysis
Don't just state a strength – *explain* it, e.g. 'Structured interviews can be large-scale and representative because they are fairly brief, so more people can be interviewed'.

Representativeness Compared with unstructured interviews, structured interviews are relatively quick to conduct. This means that a larger sample can be interviewed, which is likely to produce more representative results, allowing the researcher to make generalisations. Structured interviews have a higher response rate than mailed questionnaires and this also helps with representativeness.

Cost Because they are quick to complete, structured interviews are the cheapest form of interview. Interviewers also need only limited training.

Interviewer-interviewee contact Face-to-face interviews mean a higher response rate is likely, because the researcher's presence means that the research's purpose and importance can be explained to potential interviewees.

Limited 'interviewer effect' Interviewer effect occurs when the interviewer's presence affects the interviewee's responses and reduces validity. However, with structured interviews, interviewer effect will be far less than with open-ended, free-flowing unstructured interviews. This is because, in structured interviews, contact is limited to asking and responding to a fixed list of questions and possible answers. Some sociologists also try to minimise interviewer effect by a 'deadpan' delivery, showing no emotion, not stressing any wording etc.

Disadvantages of structured interviews

Structured interviews suffer from a number of important disadvantages, especially in relation to validity.

Lack of validity Interpretivists challenge the validity of data produced from structured interviews.

▶ Because the researcher decides the questions in advance, and because the interview schedule cannot be altered once it has been finalised, this prevents interviewees from raising new issues. The researcher has limited what the respondent can talk about and this may exclude important aspects of the research issue.

▶ Fixed-response questions may prevent the interviewee from saying what they really think – they have to force their responses to fit the researcher's categories. Anything that limits how the interviewee responds reduces the validity of the data generated.

▶ The wording of some questions may be open to interpretation and there is a limit to how far the interviewer can explain their meaning to the interviewee.

▶ It is difficult to know if the respondent is being truthful. Although this is a problem with all interviews, it is particularly so with structured interviews, since the researcher usually cannot move away from the fixed interview schedule to check the answers they are given.

▶ Structured interviews are not completely free from interviewer effect. The interviewee may interpret the interviewer's social characteristics – their age, gender, class etc – in ways that may influence their responses.

Reliability Interviewer effect may also reduce reliability because, although the same questions may be asked, interviewers are going to have different social characteristics (and the research setting will vary). Thus the interview will not be exactly replicable.

Cost Employing and training interviewers incurs a cost and even relatively brief structured interviews are not as cheap to carry out as mailed questionnaires.

Sensitive issues Asking someone a fixed list of questions in a deadpan manner can be quite off-putting and not particularly useful for investigating sensitive issues where a rapport (bond of trust and empathy) is needed.

Evaluation: how useful are structured interviews?

Positivists consider the quantitative data generated by structured interviews to be much more useful than the qualitative material that emerges from unstructured interviews. This is particularly true when the researcher wants to obtain basic factual information or gain some idea of general patterns of attitudes and behaviour.

Evaluation
Add extra evaluation by comparing interviews with another method such as observation or by comparing different types of interview.

Analysis
Explain advantages/ disadvantages, e.g. 'One interviewee, wanting to present a macho image, might understate the amount of housework he does, whereas another, hoping to represent himself as a "New Man", might overstate his true level of involvement in domestic tasks'.

Interpretation
'Examine' questions often ask about *either* strengths *or* weaknesses. Focus mainly on whichever of these the question states. Don't give a 'strengths versus weaknesses' answer.

Unstructured interviews

Unstructured interviews (sometimes called informal or focused interviews):

▶ Ask mainly open-ended questions, with no fixed set of questions to be asked of every
   respondent.

▶ Produce qualitative data because the interviewee can respond in words that are
   meaningful to them.

▶ Are guided as much by the interviewee as by the interviewer.

▶ Are informal and free-flowing, and more 'normal' than a structured interview – more like a
   guided conversation.

▶ Build a stronger relationship between researcher and research subject.

Why do interpretivists use unstructured interviews?

Interpretivists seek to discover the meanings that underlie our actions and this means using
open-ended research methods that produce valid, qualitative data. They prefer unstructured
interviews because they give people the opportunity to talk openly, unrestricted by a fixed list
of questions and possible responses. As a result it is likely that their meanings and worldview
will emerge more clearly.

However, positivists reject unstructured interviews because their lack of standardised questions
and answers means that reliable, quantitative data cannot be generated.

Validity

Interpretivists claim that the main advantage of unstructured interviews is that they create
data that is high in validity, for several reasons:

▶ The informal, conversational nature of unstructured interviews means that trust and
   rapport can develop between interviewer and interviewee. The more comfortable an
   interviewee feels, the more likely they are to 'open up'. This often helps when researching
   sensitive issues and increases the chances of getting full and honest responses.

▶ They avoid the danger of the sociologist imposing their ideas onto the interview process.
   With no set questions or fixed response categories, interviewees have the opportunity
   to reply in their own words in ways that are meaningful to them. Unlike with structured
   research techniques, the interviewee has the opportunity to raise issues they think
   are important.

▶ The flexibility of unstructured interviews also adds to validity. The interviewer can follow up
   any issues raised by the interviewee, probing more deeply to get a truer picture.

▶ Open-ended questioning allows interviewees scope to give detailed, in-depth reactions.
   The more detailed the response, the greater the likelihood of the sociologist understanding
   the research subject's worldview.

Disadvantages

Is validity achieved? Unstructured interviews may not achieve the degree of validity that is
sometimes claimed for them.

▶ The closer interviewer-interviewee bond may increase the chance of the respondent
   seeking to please by giving the answer they think the researcher wants to hear.

▶ There is also the issue of what to do with the huge amount of data that unstructured
   interviews produce. The researcher has to interpret it and be selective about what is
   presented in the final research report. In doing so, the researcher's own perspective may
   distort the interviewee's original meanings.

Application

When you use an example of a study that used unstructured interviews, don't describe the study in detail, just link it to the point you're making, e.g. 'Oakley found that informal interviews put women at ease and consequently they told her more about their experiences'.

Analysis

In an answer, when you first refer to validity, explain what it means and why it is more important to interpretivists than to positivists.

Analysis

Explain why each characteristic you identify affects validity; e.g. 'If interviewees cannot respond in the way they want to, the results will not be a true expression of their real feelings'.

Evaluation

Many students assume that unstructured interviews are 'valid' but it can be claimed that some aspects of this approach reduce validity, so point out these arguments.

Lack of reliability Positivists argue that unstructured interviews lack reliability. No fixed list of pre-set questions, plus the ability of interviewees to respond in any way they wish, makes it impossible to classify and count their responses. This means statistical evidence cannot be created from informal interviews, preventing comparisons being drawn or correlations established.

Lack of representativeness Unstructured interviews take longer to carry out and this usually limits the size of the research sample. Because it is harder to obtain a representative sample from a small number of respondents, this may limit the ability of the researcher to make generalisations.

Unsuitability for sensitive issues When answering questions about sensitive issues, some people may prefer to fill in an anonymous postal questionnaire rather than answer probing questions asked face-to-face.

Cost Interviewers need to be trained in sensitivity, the purpose of the research, how much to explain to interviewees etc. This adds to the cost, as does the fact that it takes longer to carry them out and to process the data they create. As a result, unstructured interviews are more costly than structured interviews.

Relevance The interviewee may wander off into all kinds of areas that are irrelevant to the research. Unless the interviewer is prepared to re-direct the respondent – with a possible loss of validity – a lot of time may be wasted and irrelevant data collected.

Group interviews These are usually largely unstructured and involve interviewing a group of people together. This can help jog memories, stimulate answers and suggest lines of enquiry, but there is a danger that individuals will offer conformist answers rather than say what they really think.

Evaluation: how useful are unstructured interviews?

Interpretivists have a strong preference for unstructured interviews, particularly when researching sensitive issues. However, unstructured interviews have some difficulties in achieving the degree of validity they seek.

Structured and unstructured interviewing techniques do not have to be seen as irreconcilable opposites. They can be used in a complementary way in the form of semi-structured interviews to produce both quantitative and qualitative data.

▶ A structured approach with standardised questions can be used to gather basic factual information about age, occupation, income etc.

▶ An unstructured approach with open-ended questions can be used when the researcher wants to explore interviewees' meanings and attitudes in depth.

> **Evaluation**
> When you point out a disadvantage, you can briefly attach a strength to it as evaluation, e.g. 'Although people might prefer the anonymity of questionnaires, unstructured interviews build trust and allow more in-depth questioning'.

> **Application**
> Point out that a particular study may move between types of interview, e.g. Dobash and Dobash used unstructured interviews but also asked certain questions of all interviewees.

ONE TO TRY

Question Examine the reasons why unstructured interviews are sometimes used in sociological research.   (20 marks)

Examiner's Advice There are 10 AO1 and 10 AO2 marks for this question. The focus of your answer should be on the reasons why some sociologists use unstructured interviews. You can refer to the weaknesses of this method, but only to evaluate these reasons.

You should also explain that unstructured interviews are preferred by interpretivists because the data that they create is highly valid. You can organise your reasons around theoretical, practical and ethical issues.

6 Observation

Key Issues

▶ What different types of observation do sociologists use?

▶ What are the strengths and weaknesses of each type of observation?

▶ Why do positivists prefer structured and interpretivists prefer unstructured observation?

Types of observation

▶ **Participant observation** (PO) The researcher joins in the activities of the group they are researching, involving themselves in their daily life.

▶ **Non-participant observation** The observer avoids any direct involvement with the research group, keeping a distance.

▶ **Overt observation** The researcher explains their research intention to the group, so the research subjects know they are being observed.

▶ **Covert observation** The researcher keeps their real identity and purpose secret from the research subjects. If participating, they usually pose as a genuine member of the group.

▶ **Structured observation** The researcher systematically classifies the behaviour they observe into distinct categories.

▶ **Unstructured observation** The observer simply records what they see and experience in whatever way they can.

Interpretivists tend to use overt or covert PO, recording observations in an unstructured way. Positivists tend to use structured non-participant observation.

> **Interpretation**
> If the question is about 'observation', you should cover all varieties of observation. If it is on PO or on structured observation, just stick to the type specified. Avoid slipping into non-PO if asked to examine PO (and vice versa).

Participant observation

PO varies considerably from study to study, but typical characteristics include:

▶ The observer finding a role within the group that allows them to study group behaviour.

▶ Observations are recorded in field notes.

▶ The research often involves years of fieldwork.

▶ Researchers start with an open mind and research ideas emerge during the study.

▶ It can be either covert or overt. (See below on the differences between these.)

Why do interpretivists use PO?

Interpretivists seek to discover the meanings that underlie our actions and this means using open-ended methods that produce valid, qualitative data. They find PO an effective way of uncovering people's meanings. Sustained participation in a group's activities allows the observer to gain a clear understanding of their worldview that can be constantly checked against their daily experience of the group. The researcher sees what people actually do, not what they may say they do.

However, while interpretivists consider PO to create highly valid data, positivists reject its use because they argue it lacks reliability and representativeness.

> **Application**
> Explaining the method's theoretical context is a very effective way to begin your essay. It also makes it easier to lead into use of the key concepts of validity, reliability and representativeness.

Interpretation
'Examine' questions often ask about *either* strengths *or* weaknesses. Focus mainly on whichever the question states. Don't give a 'strengths versus weaknesses' answer.

Advantages of participant observation

Validity

Interpretivists argue that PO has several features that help to produce data high in validity – that is, PO gives a true and authentic picture of the group:

▶ **Its naturalistic approach** The group is observed in its natural setting, acting normally and largely unaffected by the observer's presence (especially if using covert PO). The data is more likely to be a true account of the group's behaviour. By contrast, most other research methods are carried out in artificial situations that may alter the behaviour of those being studied.

▶ Observation of a group's normal social routines is likely to produce a more authentic account of their worldview than merely asking them questions. With questions, the researcher never knows how truthful people are being. With PO conducted over a long period, the group's 'private face' is more likely to emerge.

▶ **An open research process**. PO is a fluid, flexible approach directed less by the researcher and more by the research subjects. The researcher 'goes with the flow' of research, allowing research ideas to emerge in the process.

▶ **PO offers insight**. Only by sharing the experiences of a group can the sociologist see beneath surface appearances. Structured research (e.g. questionnaires) tends to skim over the surface of social reality, rather than developing a deeper understanding of social behaviour.

▶ **The data generated is richly detailed**. The recorded observations of participant observers have a true-to-life feel about them.

Analysis
Observation is often part of other methods, e.g. interviews and experiments, as well as being used as a main method in its own right.

Other advantages

▶ **Studying closed groups** Some social groups are difficult to research. Covert PO may well be the only way of studying a particular group or issue.

▶ **Research opportunity** PO is very flexible, so if a research opportunity suddenly occurs, the researcher can seize the chance to join and study a group.

▶ **Flexibility** If a new issue arises during a study, PO can be adapted accordingly. With structured forms of research such as formal interviews or questionnaires, new issues cannot be brought into the research process once it has started.

Analysis
It is not only criminals or 'fringe' groups such as some religious sects, but also powerful groups who may not welcome researchers intruding on them.

Disadvantages of participant observation

PO suffers from a number of disadvantages as a research method:

Unreliable and unrepresentative

▶ Positivists see PO as fundamentally flawed because it is unscientific. Being open-ended and subjective research, there is no fixed procedure and no standardised system of measurement, so the study cannot be replicated.

▶ PO gives control of the research process to the research subjects and this, with a lack of any standardised questioning, removes any chance of the data being reliable.

▶ Most PO studies are 'one-off' investigations of small social groups that are unlikely to be representative and so generalisations cannot be made from their findings.

Analysis
Don't just *state* the weaknesses (or strengths) – *explain* them; e.g. 'Most PO studies are small-scale and unrepresentative because it is impossible for a single researcher to observe more than a few people at the same time'.

Problems with validity

PO may not necessarily produce the valid data that interpretivists claim:

▶ **Hawthorne effect** The observer's presence is likely to affect the group's behaviour, particularly with overt observation. Even with covert PO, the mere presence of a new member can still influence a group's activities.

▶ **Going native** The observer may also be affected by the group, e.g. over-identifying with them. The researcher's attitude towards the group will affect their interpretation of the group's actions.

▶ **Interpretation problems** The observer can never be absolutely certain that they have understood the meaning of events in the same way as the research subjects.

Ethical issues

▶ With covert PO, the group are under the false impression that the new member is genuinely committed to the group. The group are deliberately misled and have not given their informed consent, and may even be placed in danger by the research, e.g. in Humphreys' study.

▶ The covert observer may also witness or have to participate in illegal or immoral activities, or else risk blowing their cover.

▶ With small-group PO research, it is often difficult to ensure anonymity of those being studied.

Practical problems

▶ **Getting in** – joining the group one wishes to study – can be difficult. Sometimes it is a matter of good fortune that a researcher is able to join a group, and it may depend on finding a key informant.

▶ **Staying in** may be problematic, especially if observing covertly, since it will involve maintaining a false identity and role for long periods. Writing up notes later from memory is problematic and also threatens validity. Even overt observers may find the long hours and months of intensive work stressful.

▶ **Getting out** can be difficult, especially if emotional bonds to the group have been formed.

Overt and covert PO compared

	Overt PO	**Covert PO**
Ethics	May be problem of protecting research subjects' identity.	Lack of informed consent from subjects.
Access	May be denied if group refuses to be involved in research.	Hard to gain entry – need similar social characteristics to group.
Maintaining group membership	Once accepted into group, easy to retain membership while conducting the research.	Constant risk of cover being 'blown'. Discovery means end of research and possibly personal danger.
Asking questions	Can openly question members to clarify points so validity may increase.	Direct questions can raise suspicions - restricts observer from checking meanings.
Validity of data	Group members may act differently (Hawthorne effect), so not a true picture of the group's behaviour.	Group acts normally, so data is more valid.

Evaluation
If the question is about weaknesses, use a strength to evaluate one or two of the weaknesses, e.g. 'Although covert PO has ethical problems, it is sometimes the only way to study certain social groups such as criminals'.

Application
Avoid describing a particular study at length. Instead, use any examples of PO simply to illustrate the specific practical, ethical or theoretical strengths or weaknesses you identify.

Evaluation: how useful is PO?

▶ PO lacks reliability and representativeness, but interpretivists are more interested in validity and they see PO as the technique that gets closest to this aim. However, it is doubtful whether even this approach can produce research evidence that is completely valid.

▶ PO has a particular strength in that it is sometimes the only way to study certain groups and issues, such as deviant behaviour.

Structured observation

Structured observation uses an observation schedule to identify and measure patterns of behaviour. The researcher decides in advance how to categorise the behaviour they will observe. The categories on the schedule are coded so that the data collected can be easily counted and turned into statistics. For example, the researcher might record the frequency of events such as teachers disciplining pupils. Recording of observations may take place every five seconds or so. It is hard for a researcher to conceal that they are using an observation schedule, so structured observation is usually overt.

Application
Remember the importance of putting a method in its theoretical context. Doing this at the start of your essay is a very effective way to begin.

Why do positivists use structured observation?

Positivists argue that there is a measurable, objective social reality 'out there'. They take a scientific approach using standardised methods of research to obtain quantitative data that allows them to produce generalisations and cause-and-effect statements. Positivists prefer to use structured observation because it uses fixed categories and so observations can be easily quantified.

Advantages and disadvantages

Evaluation
Structured observation has been used extensively in educational research because it is very suitable for measuring classroom interaction.

Reliability Structured observation produces reliable data because observations can be easily replicated by other researchers using the same fixed categories as the original researcher.

Comparing data Structured observation allows quantitative data to be produced quickly and easily, simply by counting the frequency or duration of the events that are observed. This means the results of different observations can be directly compared, enabling the researcher to see patterns and relationships.

Loss of validity

▶ Counting the frequency of events doesn't tell us about their meaning.

▶ Events may not fit any of the categories, or may overlap several categories.

▶ Different observers may place the same event into different categories.

▶ The observer cannot always observe and record everything that is going on in an interaction.

Other problems Structured observation is only useful in studying small-scale interactions. It is also a very intensive method to carry out.

ONE TO TRY

Question Examine the strengths that sociologists see in using observation in their research. (20 marks)

Examiner's Advice There are 10 AO1 and 10 AO2 marks for this question. The focus of your answer should be on the strengths of observation. You can refer to the weaknesses of observation, but only to evaluate its strengths. You need to be careful here as there are several forms of observation (overt and covert, structured and unstructured, participant and non-participant) and each has different strengths.

You should also explain that unstructured participant observation is preferred by interpretivists, while structured observation is seen as having many strengths by positivists.

7 Official Statistics

Key Issues
▶ What types of official statistics do sociologists use?
▶ What are the strengths and weaknesses of official statistics?
▶ Why do positivists prefer to use official statistics?

What are official statistics?

Official statistics are quantitative data collected by government bodies. They come from two main sources – the day-to-day activities of government departments, and surveys like the Census. We can distinguish between:

▶ **'Hard' statistics** Simple counts that register events such as births and deaths. These are not easily manipulated.

▶ **'Soft' statistics** These are more easily manipulated, e.g. crime statistics.

Most of the strengths and weaknesses of official statistics come from the fact that they are secondary data, so the collection processes are not in the sociologist's control.

Why do positivists use official statistics?

Positivists start from the assumption that there is a measurable objective social reality. They take a scientific approach using standardised research methods to obtain quantitative data that allows them to produce generalisations and cause-and-effect statements. They prefer official statistics because these deliver large-scale, representative, quantitative data, collected by reliable methods such as questionnaires. However, interpretivists reject their use because they see them as socially constructed and lacking validity.

Advantages of official statistics

Availability As they are already in existence, they are cheap and readily available in an accessible form. Some statistics are published monthly, most annually, and so can be analysed for trends. The data is already categorised and in immediately usable form.

Representativeness Official statistics are usually based on a very large sample, so they are often highly representative, e.g. divorce and marriage registration. The ten-yearly Census gives virtually complete coverage of all households in the UK. Statistics created from government surveys may be somewhat less representative because they use smaller samples, but still much larger ones than sociologists can normally obtain.

Coverage They cover most important aspects of social life, especially those the state is interested in, e.g. education, divorce, crime etc.

Prompts to research They can provide the starting point for research, e.g. by revealing a new pattern needing further investigation. Boys' educational underachievement was first identified from official statistics.

Background data They often provide useful background material, e.g. about the ethnic, class and gender make-up of a research group.

Comparability of data Their quantitative nature makes it easy to draw comparisons and identify trends, e.g. in the number of divorces, household composition, rates of domestic violence.

Analysis Distinguish between 'hard' and 'soft' statistics in your opening paragraph. Keep referring to this distinction throughout your answer.

Analysis Don't just *state* strengths or weaknesses: *explain why* they are strengths or weaknesses – e.g. 'official statistics are usually large-scale and representative because government wants to know what is happening in society as a whole'.

Analysis Point out aspects of social life that are well covered by official statistics – and those that aren't.

Application Avoid describing a particular example of official statistics at length (e.g. the Census). Instead, connect examples to the strengths or weaknesses you identify.

Reliability Because the same categories and mode of collection are usually used each time the statistics are gathered, the research can be replicated by others. The basis on which the statistics have been collected is also usually publicly stated, so sociologists can check whether the same procedures have been followed each time they are gathered.

Problems with official statistics

Evaluation
If the question is about weaknesses, use a strength to evaluate one or two of the weaknesses, e.g. 'although official statistics are open to political manipulation, the way they are collected is open to public scrutiny so this manipulation can be identified'.

Definition and measurement Definitions of the concepts used, how they have been operationalised and how the data is presented may differ from those of the sociologist. For example, official statistics measure class in terms of occupation, whereas some sociologists see class as based on ownership or non-ownership of property.

Reliability Official statistics may not be as reliable as positivists claim. Even in the Census, recording errors are made and households missed out, and people may complete forms inaccurately.

Social construction Interpretivists argue that official statistics are social constructs, not objective 'truth' – the result of a social process of negotiation. For example, for a crime to appear in the official statistics, it has to be observed, reported and recorded. Each decision in this process (by victims, police etc) affects what gets officially included as a 'crime'. Victim surveys reveal the official crime statistics to be an underestimate.

Interpretation
'Examine' questions usually ask about *either* strengths *or* weaknesses. Focus mainly on whichever the question states. Don't give a 'strengths versus weaknesses' answer.

Political bias Marxists claim official statistics are not politically neutral, but reflect ruling-class interests and ideology. The definitions used, areas of social life covered and how statistics are presented are all political decisions. For example, the official definition of unemployment altered over thirty times in the 1980s, massaging the total downwards and presenting the government in a more positive light.

Male bias Feminists argue official statistics are biased against women, e.g. definitions of 'work' used in the Census exclude unpaid housework. Women are also more likely to be 'counted out' in unemployment figures.

Evaluation: how useful are official statistics?

Positivists often present them as 'social facts', but interpretivists see them as social constructs, not true representations of reality.

'Hard' statistics are less socially constructed and more accurate, because they are simple counts of events (such as births and deaths). However, 'soft' statistics (such as crime or unemployment statistics) are less reliable and less valid because they are more easily manipulated politically or are the outcome of interactions and labelling.

> **ONE TO TRY**
>
> **Question** Examine the reasons why some sociologists do not use official statistics in their research.   (20 marks)
>
> **Examiner's Advice** There are 10 AO1 and 10 AO2 marks for this question. The focus of your answer should be on the problems of official statistics. You can refer to the strengths of this source of data, but only to evaluate these reasons. You should identify the different types of official statistics including 'hard' and 'soft' statistics. Give examples of each. You should also explain that official statistics are criticised by interpretivists who argue they are socially constructed and lack validity. You can organise your reasons into theoretical, practical and ethical issues.

8 Documents

Key Issues

▶ What kinds of documents do sociologists use?

▶ What are the strengths and weaknesses of different types of documents?

What are documents?

Documents are secondary data created by individuals, groups and organisations, that sociologists may find useful in their research. We can distinguish between:

▶ **Personal documents** such as letters, diaries, memoirs, autobiographies, notes and photo collections.

▶ **Public documents** such as reports from governments, charities and businesses.

Documents contain mainly qualitative data that expresses the beliefs and meanings held by individuals and organisations. However, some documents contain statistical data as well, e.g. the Black Report into health inequalities. Some documents are contemporary, others give historical perspective.

Why do interpretivists use documents?

Interpretivists seek to discover the meanings that underlie our actions and this means using open-ended research methods that produce valid, qualitative data. Most documents meet interpretivists' requirement that data should be qualitative and allow the researcher to explore the meanings people attach to events. Interpretivists regard documents as high in validity because they are the freely expressed meanings of those who produce them.

However, positivists mainly reject their use because they consider that they lack reliability and representativeness. Nevertheless, positivists may make use of the statistical data contained in some documents, or may convert the qualitative contents of documents into quantitative data by using content analysis.

Personal documents

These take the form of diaries, memoirs, autobiographies and letters created by individuals for a variety of uses.

Advantages

▶ Mostly written for personal purposes, these often have a fairly high degree of validity and provide a genuine insight into people's attitudes.

▶ Most personal documents are also cheap and save the researcher time, although accessing them is not always straightforward.

Disadvantages

Personal documents may have many problems that can make it difficult to evaluate their validity.

▶ Some groups (e.g. the illiterate) are unlikely to produce personal documents such as letters and diaries and so their views are not represented, while those with the necessary time and literacy skills may be over-represented.

▶ Some documents are created after the event with the benefit of hindsight, e.g. memoirs and autobiographies.

▶ Personal documents such as letters are written with an audience in mind and this may affect what is recorded. Personal bias is also likely to be present.

Interpretation
Does the question ask about personal, public or all kinds of documents? If the question is about documents in general, then cover all varieties; if it is on a particular type, only cover that type. Give examples and point out their specific strengths or weaknesses.

Analysis
Don't just *state* weaknesses (or strengths), *explain* them – e.g. 'Diaries give valid data because they are not usually written for public consumption and so the writer is more likely to be honest in what they write'.

Evaluation
If the question is about weaknesses, use a strength to evaluate one or two of the weaknesses – e.g. 'Although historical documents give the researcher an insight into the way people see their world, they are often unrepresentative, as many social groups in the past were illiterate'.

Public documents

▶ Produced by bodies such as government, business, the media and voluntary organisations, these documents are often plentiful, detailed, cheap and easy to access. For example, there are government reports on all areas of social policy.

▶ However, because their authors are aware that the documents are publicly available, the content is likely to be selective and presented with a particular bias. For example, media reports may reflect the political views of the journalist or media owner.

Historical documents

Historical documents are often the only way in which we can study past societies, especially if there are no longer any survivors whom we could question. However, there can be particular problems interpreting historical documents, e.g. because the meaning of words changes over time. Some historical documents may be lost or destroyed, giving an incomplete and unrepresentative picture of the past.

Content analysis

Quantitative content analysis of documents measures the amount of coverage given to a particular issue, e.g. news reports can be quantified in terms of the amount of time/space given to particular points of view. However, simply knowing how much coverage there is of something doesn't tell us about its meaning. Therefore interpretivists use qualitative content analysis to examine the meanings attached to particular words and images. However, this has the problem of interpretation and different researchers may interpret the same statement or image differently.

Testing the usefulness of documents

John Scott (1990) suggests four tests of any document:

▶ **Authenticity** Is it genuine? Is it what it claims to be?

▶ **Credibility** Can we believe the document and the sincerity of the author?

▶ **Representativeness** How typical is the document of a wider social group?

▶ **Meaning** Can we interpret the author's meanings correctly?

Evaluation: how useful are documents?

Documents can provide insights into social behaviour that are useful to sociologists, particularly those who accept the need to explore the meanings social actors attach to events. They can provide a historical or 'insider' perspective.

However, they are limited in terms of availability, representativeness and lack of systematisation, and they may not cover all areas of sociological interest. They are therefore rarely the main element in a study (other than historical studies), but they often contribute an important dimension to research.

Question Examine the weaknesses of different types of documents used in sociological research. (20 marks)

Examiner's Advice There are 10 AO1 and 10 AO2 marks for this question. The focus of your answer should be on the weaknesses of different types of documents. You can refer to the strengths of this method but only to evaluate these weaknesses. You should identify the range of different documents used by sociologists, e.g. public, personal and historical. Give examples of each.

ONE TO TRY

You should also explain that the use of documents is criticised by positivists for being unreliable and unrepresentative. You can organise your answer into theoretical, practical and ethical weaknesses.

9 Methods in Context

Key Issues

▶ How can each method be applied to the investigation of a particular research issue in education?

▶ What are the strengths and limitations of each method for studying particular research issues in education?

Using experiments to study education

Application in the classroom

Sociologists sometimes use field experiments to study aspects of classroom life such as teacher expectations and pupils' self-concepts. The classroom has clear boundaries in terms of both space and time. This makes it easier for the researcher to achieve a degree of control over the situation and develop an effective field experiment. Several researchers have also used laboratory experiments to investigate teacher expectations.

Experiments have been used to study educational issues such as:

▶ **Teacher expectations**

▶ **Classroom interaction**

▶ **Labelling**

▶ **Pupils' self-concepts.**

These issues can be examined in small-scale contexts that have clear physical and social boundaries, such as classrooms.

Reliability

Experiments are often relatively simple and therefore easy to repeat. Although experiments in educational settings may not be exactly replicable, schools have broadly similar features and so experiments can still be repeated in broadly similar ways, e.g. the original 'Pygmalion in the Classroom' study has been repeated hundreds of times.

Ethical problems

Some experiments have used pupils in real learning situations. However, there are particular ethical issues with carrying out experiments on young people. They are more vulnerable and are less able to understand what is happening to them, and therefore less able to give informed consent. Laboratory experiments are rarely used in educational research for these reasons.

Limited application

Experiments are small-scale and can usually only examine a single aspect of behaviour. Larger issues in education, such as social class and achievement, cannot easily be studied using this method.

Experiments are generally less useful for investigating educational issues such as:

▶ **Gender and achievement**

▶ **Education policy**

▶ **Selection and segregation.**

These issues are large-scale topics that are hard to replicate in a laboratory or to find a suitable real-life situation to manipulate in a field experiment.

Controlling all the variables

Experiments require researchers to control the variables in the situation. However, schools are large, complex institutions and many variables affect the behaviour of teachers and pupils, e.g. class size, streaming, type of school. It is impossible even to identify, let alone control, all the variables that might exert an influence on teachers' expectations.

Using questionnaires to study education

Practical issues

Questionnaires are very useful for gathering large quantities of basic information quickly and cheaply from large numbers of pupils, teachers or educational establishments. Researchers can use questionnaires to correlate factors such as achievement, attendance and behaviour with variables such as school size, class size and number of staff.

Sampling frames

Schools are a good source of ready-made sampling frames. They keep lists of pupils and staff, and these can provide accurate sampling frames from which to draw a representative sample. Schools also have ready-made opportunity samples of pupils and teachers, e.g. class lists.

Response rate

Response rates for questionnaires are often low. However, when conducted in schools, response rates can be higher than in other areas. Once a head teacher has put their authority behind the research, teachers and pupils may be under pressure to cooperate. Pupils, teachers and parents are also accustomed to completing questionnaires issued by the school, such as student satisfaction surveys.

Researching pupils

Children generally have a shorter attention span than adults and so a short questionnaire can be more effective than lengthy interviews. However, this limits the amount of information that can be gathered. Pupils with poor literacy skills may be unable or unwilling to complete questionnaires.

Operationalising concepts

Turning abstract ideas such as 'deferred gratification' into a measurable form is particularly difficult when researching pupils. Young people have a poorer grasp of abstract ideas, so they are less likely to understand some of the researcher's questions.

Samples

Schools may not keep lists that reflect the researcher's interests, e.g. the researcher may wish to investigate ethnicity, but the school may not keep lists of pupils sorted by their ethnic origin.

Validity

The life experiences of children (especially primary-age children) are narrower, so they may not actually know the answers to questions. Consequently, questionnaires may be of little value.

Using structured interviews to study education

Response rate

Structured interviews usually take less time than unstructured interviews and so they are less disruptive to schools' activities. Therefore researchers are more likely to receive official support for the research. The hierarchical nature of the school may then work in their favour and this may increase the response rate.

Reliability

Structured interviews are easy to replicate. Therefore large-scale patterns in educational behaviour can be identified, e.g. in gender and subject choice.

Validity

As young people tend to have better verbal than literacy skills, interviews may be more successful than written questionnaires as a method of obtaining valid answers. However, the formal nature of structured interviews (similar to exams, lessons and other controlled school situations) means pupils are unlikely to feel at ease and therefore may be less forthcoming.

Structured interviews are generally less useful for investigating educational issues such as:

▶ **Classroom interaction**

▶ **The official curriculum.**

These issues are topics that require either direct observation or an examination of formal documentation.

Question design

It is more difficult to create questions for use with young people because their linguistic and intellectual skills are not fully developed. As a result, they may not understand long, complex sentences or some abstract concepts. In answers, they may have a more limited vocabulary and use words incorrectly. They therefore need more help and clarification – neither of which happens in structured interviews.

Ethical issues

Parental permission may be required to interview children. Whether or not this is given depends partly on the sensitivity of the research topic, e.g. sex education.

Power and status differences

Pupils and teachers are not equal in power and status, and this affects their behaviour. Pupils often alter their responses to seek adult approval by giving untrue but socially acceptable answers. Children see adults as authority figures, so the researcher may come across as a 'teacher in disguise'. This is particularly true in formal interview situations. This will reduce the validity of the interview data.

Unstructured interviews have been used to study educational issues such as:

▶ **Teachers' 'racialised expectations' about pupils**

▶ **Pupil subcultures**

▶ **Parental attitudes**

▶ **How school policies are actually implemented in practice.**

These issues involve finding out the meanings and attitudes people hold, so in-depth, open-ended questioning is more appropriate.

Using unstructured interviews to study education

Power and status inequality

Unstructured interviews may overcome barriers of power and status inequality. Their informality can establish rapport more easily. Labov's research shows that unstructured interviews can encourage interviewees to open up and respond more fully. This produces more valid data. This can be particularly useful when dealing with sensitive topics such as bullying.

Practical issues

Pupils may be inarticulate or reluctant to talk, so unstructured interviews give them time, space and encouragement to work out their responses. However, younger pupils have a shorter attention span, so they may find long unstructured interviews too demanding.

Validity

The difficulties in communicating with young people mean that unstructured interviews may be suitable, because the interviewer can clear up misunderstandings by explaining questions.

However, children may also have more difficulty in keeping to the point and may present contradictory or irrelevant responses to the questions.

Unstructured interviews are generally less useful for investigating educational issues such as:

▶ **Patterns of achievement**

▶ **Speech codes used in the classroom.**

These issues are either large-scale topics or they require the detailed recording of actual events.

Reliability

To put young people at ease, some interviewers try to maintain a relaxed atmosphere by nodding, smiling and making eye contact. However, this cannot be standardised, so different interviewers may obtain very different results and this would reduce the reliability of their findings.

Social desirability

Pupils are accustomed to adults 'knowing better' and so may defer to them in interviews. Children are more likely than adults to change their original answer when the question is repeated because they think it must have been wrong. Teachers may seek to protect their professional self-image and so are likely to represent themselves in the most positive light. However, an unstructured interview allows researchers to probe behind this image.

Interviewer training

Unstructured interviewing of young people requires more training than interviewing adults. Interviewers need to be trained not to interrupt children's answers, to tolerate long pauses and to avoid repeating questions, since this may make children change their original answer for fear that it was wrong.

Using structured observation to study education

Practical issues

As a relatively closed physical and social environment, the classroom is well suited to structured observation. It is relatively easy for an observer to sit at the back of a classroom recording behaviour into set categories. The short duration of most lessons also means that the observer does not get fatigued. The relative simplicity of structured observational methods in the classroom means that they are quicker, cheaper and require less training than many other methods.

However, some school situations (e.g. playground activity) often involve too many different behaviours to be satisfactorily categorised.

Reliability

The range of classroom behaviours (of both teachers and pupils) is relatively limited and therefore a limited number of behaviour categories can easily be established for use in the observation. It is therefore easy to replicate classroom observations. Structured observation also generates quantitative data, which makes comparison straightforward.

Validity

Interpretivists criticise structured observation of classroom interaction for its lack of validity. Simply counting classroom behaviour and classifying it into a limited number of pre-determined categories ignores the meanings that pupils and teachers attach to it.

Observer presence

The presence of a stranger, probably non-participant, observing behaviour using a checklist can be very off-putting (and certainly difficult to disguise) in a school. This is likely to affect teachers' and pupils' behaviour and reduce validity.

Using participant observation to study education

Validity

Participant observation is more likely to overcome the problem of status differences between pupils and researcher, thus allowing the researcher to gain acceptance by pupils, resulting in more valid data. Nevertheless, both teachers and pupils are skilled at altering their behaviour when being observed by those in authority. This makes it difficult for researchers to know if the behaviour they are seeing in schools is genuine.

Structured observation has been used to study educational issues such as:

▶ **Classroom interaction**

▶ **Teachers' 'racialised expectations' of pupils**

▶ **Labelling**

▶ **Gender and classroom behaviour.**

These issues can be examined in small-scale contexts that have clear physical and social boundaries, such as classrooms.

Structured observation is generally less useful for investigating educational issues such as:

▶ **Class and achievement**

▶ **Education policy**

▶ **Material deprivation and achievement.**

These issues are either large-scale topics or are difficult to observe.

Participant observation has been used to study educational issues such as:

▶ **Classroom interaction**

▶ **Teachers' 'racialised expectations' about pupils**

▶ **Gender and the 'male gaze'**

▶ **Pupil subcultures.**

These issues can be examined in small-scale contexts such as classrooms that have clear physical and social boundaries.

Practical issues

Schools are complex places and it may take an observer weeks or even months to understand how a school functions. Classroom observation may be less disruptive than interviews, so it may be easier to gain permission to observe lessons than to interview pupils and teachers. However, observation is restricted by the school timetable, holidays, the head teacher's control over access etc. There is not much privacy in a school – they are very busy places, so recording observations can be problematic.

Ethical issues

Pupils are more vulnerable than adults and may not be able to give informed consent. This means that classroom observation normally has to be overt. There are also greater ethical issues when dealing with schools in terms of protecting the school's identity. A poor public image as a result of the research can damage a school's reputation and the education of its pupils.

The Hawthorne effect

Most observation has to be overt – there are few 'cover' roles the researcher can adopt because he or she stands out as being much older than the pupils. The Hawthorne effect is therefore unavoidable to some degree. Teachers may be suspicious of an observer in their classroom and alter their normal behaviour.

Representativeness

Participant observation of schools and classrooms can only be carried out on a very small scale. The education system is vast, with over 35,000 schools and colleges. This makes representativeness virtually impossible to achieve using this method.

Using official statistics to study education

Practical issues

The government collects statistics from over 35,000 schools in England and Wales. This saves sociologists time and money, as well as allowing them to make comparisons, e.g. between the achievements of different social classes, ethnic groups or genders. Statistics also allow us to examine trends over time, e.g. in achievement or attendance. Governments are interested in many of the same educational issues as sociologists, e.g. subject choice, racism in schools, and inequality of achievement, so the statistics produced by government are likely to be very useful to researchers.

However, the official definitions of key concepts and issues may differ from those that sociologists use, e.g. measuring achievement by 5 A*-C grades at GCSE.

Representativeness

Some official statistics on education are highly representative, e.g. all state schools have to complete a school census three times a year. It would be impossible for researchers to collect this quantity and range of data themselves. These statistics cover virtually every pupil in the country, so they are highly representative.

Reliability

The government uses standard definitions and categories in the collection of educational statistics. The same collection process is replicated from year to year, allowing direct comparisons to be made, e.g. of exam performance. However, governments may change the definitions and categories, e.g. several definitions of 'value added' have been used to measure school performance. This reduces reliability.

Participant observation is generally less useful for investigating educational issues such as:
- Class and achievement
- Education policy
- Material deprivation and achievement.

These issues are large-scale topics; observation of small groups is likely to produce unrepresentative data.

Official statistics have been used to study educational issues such as:
- Class and achievement
- Education policy
- Material deprivation and achievement.

These issues are large-scale topics on which governments collect nationwide statistics.

Official statistics are generally less useful for investigating educational issues such as:
- Classroom interaction
- Teachers' 'racialised expectations' of pupils
- Labelling
- Gender and classroom behaviour.

These issues are small-scale topics on which governments generally do not keep statistical data.

Validity

Interpretivists challenge the validity of educational statistics, seeing them as socially constructed, e.g. pupil attendance statistics are the outcome of definitions and decisions made by parents, teachers and pupils. Schools may manipulate their statistical records because there is pressure on them to present themselves positively in order to maintain their funding and parental support. This undermines the validity of the statistics. However, some educational statistics are less open to manipulation, e.g. pupil numbers on roll and exam results.

Using documents to study education

Practical issues

Because most education is run by the state and because schools and colleges compete with each other for 'customers', a large amount of information about education is made publicly available. This includes school policy statements, local authority guidelines, school brochures and websites. Other documents include minutes of staff meetings and working parties, and pupils' reports.

Ethical issues

There are few ethical concerns with public documents produced by schools because they have been placed in the public domain. There are more ethical problems with using personal documents such as school reports, pupils' workbooks, teachers' diaries etc.

Reliability

Many school documents, e.g. attendance registers, are in a systematic format and so researchers can draw direct comparisons. However, accidental mistakes made when completing these documents reduce their reliability.

Credibility

Public documents give the 'official' picture of what is happening in a school or college. In an education market, schools want to present themselves in the most positive way and so many documents are constructed with a parental audience in mind. This makes them less believable and less valid.

Representativeness

Because some documents are legally required of all schools and colleges, they are likely to be representative. However, not all behaviour is recorded (e.g. racist incidents) and this reduces representantiveness. Personal documents produced by pupils or teachers are often less representative because they are collected in an unsystematic way.

Validity

Documents can provide important insights into the meanings held by teachers and pupils and can therefore be high in validity. However, all documents are open to different interpretations. Age and other differences between the researcher and pupils mean that the researcher cannot be sure that their interpretation of the meaning of pupils' personal documents is accurate.

Documents have been used to study educational issues such as:

▶ **Education in the past**

▶ **Stereotyping in school books**

▶ **The official curriculum.**

These issues require either a historical viewpoint, or the analysis of written or other texts.

Documents are generally less useful for investigating educational issues such as:

▶ **Working-class experiences of schooling**

▶ **Classroom interaction**

▶ **Labelling.**

These issues would require documents to have been created by those involved, which is unlikely to be the case.

Practice question and student answer

> ### Question
> Examine the advantages of using surveys in sociological research.   (20 marks)

Student Answer by Rosie

Surveys have many uses in sociological research, for example, they can cover issues on a large scale and anonymity means that sensitive issues can be explored. They can also be used to create a lot of quantitative data from which patterns of behaviour can be seen. Surveys can take several forms, the most common of which is the questionnaire. An alternative is to use structured interviews.

Questionnaires have the strength of being more representative. Because they can be carried out using a large research population, there is a greater chance of getting representative responses. This allows researchers to make generalisations from their results. However, a low response rate from those sent out damages the representativeness of the results of the questionnaire. Only one type of person may have answered, for example, the elderly or housewives with time to spare.

Questionnaires are also very useful for getting responses from a geographically widespread population. Posting out surveys or emailing them, means that people from the whole country can be contacted. This again may lead to a more representative response. However, when questionnaires are mailed out to people's homes, researchers can never be certain that the person it was sent to was the person who filled it out. This then affects the validity and reliability of the results.

The researcher is not around when the questionnaire is completed so unlike with interviews or observation, there is no chance that their presence will affect how the survey is answered. This improves the validity of the responses as the person filling in the questionnaire will put the answers that they want without being influenced by the sociologist. However, it also means that questions cannot be clarified by the researcher, which may lead to misunderstandings and invalid answers.

Surveys, especially questionnaires, have fewer ethical problems. If a respondent does not want to be involved, then they can simply not return the questionnaire or walk away from the interview. Questionnaires may also be better when dealing with sensitive issues involving personal experiences or breaking the law. The fact that they are anonymous means that people can be perfectly honest without fear of any bad consequences. However, respondents may still lie as they may not trust the researcher to preserve their anonymity.

This is a sound way to begin an answer. Rosie outlines a few advantages and starts to unpack what 'surveys' are.

This is an example of both analysis and evaluation – Rosie doesn't just state the strength of representativeness, she explains why surveys can achieve this, then she questions whether this is actually the case.

Many students fall into the trap of linking reliability and validity without showing the examiner that they know the difference between these two very different concepts. It is a good general rule never to link the two together in an answer.

Some analysis (through explanation) and, in the last sentence, some evaluation makes this an effective paragraph. It is a good idea to put in an alternative or a criticism in the last sentence of a paragraph to gain evaluation marks.

This is an effective paragraph which explains and questions a set of apparent advantages. However, Rosie could still expand on the ethical aspects of questionnaires.

> There is also some analysis through explanation here as well as some evaluation.

> This final paragraph has the appearance of being a conclusion but in reality has no content. This statement could be made of any method by just changing the method name.

Surveys are probably better for gathering basic information about attitudes – complex subjects cannot be easily studied with questionnaires as they never go into enough depth for a full and complete sociological understanding. Because too much time would be spent analysing detailed responses to open questions, questionnaires generally use questions that require simpler answers. The result is that answers can be easily turned into statistical data. The researcher can then see connections for example, between gender and educational achievement.

So in conclusion, surveys are a useful method of sociological research but the many problems discussed above can affect their reliability, representativeness and validity.

12/20

How to turn this into a top-mark answer

First of all, Rosie's answer is not a bad one! Not much extra is needed to improve it to 16+/20. It already has some analysis (through explanation) and some evaluation. Crucially, Rosie does not spend a lot of her essay on the weaknesses of surveys – this would have used up a lot of time for very limited reward. There are a number of things that Rosie could do to increase her mark and take her essay into the top mark band. Three things in particular would make a big difference.

Theoretical location

This answer makes no mention at all of theory. Rosie's answer would have been a lot stronger if she had explained why surveys are strongly favoured by positivists for their reliability and representativeness because of their fixed questions, large scale etc. Pointing out whether or not a method is favoured by positivists or interpretivists is an excellent way to begin an answer to 'Examine' questions.

Using concepts accurately

Rosie's use of the key concepts of reliability, representativeness and validity is sometimes accurate, sometimes not accurate. In particular, she uses reliability and validity interchangeably. Rosie needs to improve her understanding of what each concept means.

Covering other forms of surveys

The answer mainly focuses on questionnaires and would have benefited from a little more about structured interviews. This would make for a more balanced answer.

Practice Paper for Unit 1

Read Items A and B and answer parts (a) to (e) below.

Item A

According to functionalists, the modern family benefits its individual members and society as a whole, by performing positive functions for everyone. This enables them to continue to perform their social roles and thus play their part in maintaining the social system.

However, feminists reject this as a false view of family life. They argue that the instrumental and expressive roles functionalists identify for spouses are not only different but also unequal. In their view, the traditional family is patriarchal and oppresses women. This is one reason why households other than the nuclear family are on the increase.

Item B

The common media image of the family is that of the *nuclear* family – a married heterosexual couple and their biological children. However, while this is widely thought of as the 'typical' family in the United Kingdom today, some sociologists argue that the nuclear family is no longer the norm. They point to changes that have taken place in the last 40 or 50 years, such as the increase in the number of lone parent families and cohabiting couples.

However, others argue that such changes are exaggerated. If we take a life cycle approach, we find that although most people at any one time are not in a nuclear family, most people will spend a significant part of their lives in a fairly conventional nuclear family.

(a) Explain the difference between a household and a family (**Item A**).   (4 marks)

(b) Explain the difference between the instrumental role and the expressive role (**Item A**).   (4 marks)

(c) Identify **two** ways in which women may be oppressed in the family (**Item A**).   (4 marks)

(d) Examine the reasons for changes in the birth rate over the last century.   (24 marks)

(e) Using material from **Item B** and elsewhere, assess the claim that the nuclear family has ceased to be the norm for family life in the United Kingdom today.   (24 marks)

Practice Paper for Unit 2

Question 1   Read Item A and answer parts (a) to (d) below.

Item A

Functionalists argue that it is crucial to society's survival that it has a set of agreed values – a value consensus. Education is central to the maintenance of this consensus. Schools socialise young people into society's core values, which in most western countries are values such as individual achievement and meritocracy. Thus for functionalists, the main function of education is to maintain value consensus.

Marxists disagree that there is such a value consensus and argue that schools socialise young people into the values of a ruling class.

(a) Explain what is meant by an 'education market'.   (2 marks)

(b) Identify **three** reasons why female and male pupils often choose different subjects in school.   (6 marks)

(c) Outline some of the sociological explanations as to why some pupils form anti-school subcultures.
                                                                                                       (12 marks)

(d) Using material from **Item A** and elsewhere, assess the view that the main function of education is to maintain value consensus.   (20 marks)

Question 2   Read Item B and answer the question that follows.

Item B

Researching teachers' attitudes towards male and female pupils

Sociologists are interested in investigating how far, and in what ways, teachers hold different expectations of male and female pupils. As these expectations are likely to affect the way teachers act towards male and female pupils, they may well contribute to gender differences in exam results and subject choice.

Some sociologists use participant observation to study teacher interaction with pupils of both genders. This has the advantage of enabling them to see how teachers actually treat pupils in the classroom. However, there is the problem that teachers are very aware that they have a professional role to maintain. Furthermore, classrooms pose particular problems of access for observers.

Alternatively, some sociologists use questionnaires that are completed by those involved in classroom interactions. Their anonymity means that the issue of professional role maintenance is less of a problem. However, the sensitive nature of teacher expectations of male and female pupils may still cause problems.

Using material from **Item B** and elsewhere, assess the strengths and weaknesses of using one of the methods below to research teachers' attitudes towards male and female pupils:

Either (i) participant observation;
Or (ii) questionnaires.   (20 marks)

Question 3

(a) Explain what is meant by a 'longitudinal study'.   (2 marks)

(b) Suggest **two** problems sociologists find when using field experiments in their research.   (4 marks)

(c) Identify **two** sampling techniques used by sociologists in their research.   (4 marks)

(d) Examine the advantages of using structured interviews in sociological research.   (20 marks)

Top Marks Answers for Unit 1

The answers below to the Practice Paper questions on page 84 all scored full marks.

Answer

(a) A household is one person living alone or a group of people who live together. They don't have to be related (e.g. three students sharing a flat). A family is a group of people who are related by blood or marriage.

(b) The instrumental role is the breadwinner, whereas the expressive role is the nurturer.

(c) A woman may be oppressed in the family by the use of male domestic violence, and because her domestic labour is unpaid.

> **Examiner's Comments**
> Three clear, accurate and concise answers. Note that these can be quite brief and yet still score full marks.

(d) The birth rate is the number of babies born per year, per thousand of the population. It is currently around 11. However, it has changed significantly over the course of the last century. In 1900, it was much higher – about 29. And although the long-term trend has been downwards, the rate has fluctuated considerably. For example, there have been three 'baby booms' – one after each world war, and another in the 1960s. The rate fluctuated after this and then increased after 2001.

There are many reasons for the changes in the birth rate. The postwar baby booms were the result of postponed marriages, creating a 'backlog' of births. More recently, the birth rate has been lower because women are waiting longer to have children, which means some will be too old to have many, and more are choosing to remain childless. Underlying these trends are changes in women's position.

Women today are better educated and have more career opportunities, while feminist ideas have raised their aspirations. This gives them an alternative to just being housewives and mothers, so they choose to have fewer children in order to develop their careers. Also, 'family unfriendly' policies by employers make it difficult to combine a career and motherhood. Easier access to reliable contraception also means fewer births.

Another reason is the fall in the infant mortality rate (IMR) – the number of babies who die under the age of one year, per 1,000 live births. This has fallen from over 150 to about 5 since 1900. Where many infants die, parents have more to 'compensate', pushing up the birth rate. Behind the fall in the IMR are factors such as better nutrition, hygiene, sanitation, housing and health services. Since the 1950s, medical factors have become more important, e.g. antibiotics and mass immunisation against childhood diseases.

Economic and legal factors are also important. Until the late 19th century, children were an economic asset as they could be sent to work from an early age. As children have been excluded from the labour market by child labour laws and compulsory schooling, so they have become an economic liability, with parents having to support them for many years. This is an incentive to have fewer children.

Cultural factors are also important. Ariès argues that the 20th century was 'the century of the child', i.e. Western society and the family are now 'child-centred' – the focus is on the child's interests and well being as never before. One consequence is that parents now focus on 'quality' rather than 'quantity' – they have fewer children but invest more in them emotionally and financially. Thus the way childhood is constructed nowadays lowers the birth rate.

One final factor is demographic. As the average age of the population rises, the proportion of potential parents (i.e. young, fertile people) declines. The average age of the UK population is now nearly 40. Overall, the reasons for the change in the birth rate, notably its long-term downward trend, are complex and often inter-related. $24/24$

> **Examiner's Comments**
> This is a thorough, well-focused answer covering a range of reasons. Each one is analysed and explained clearly and fully, often exploring the 'reasons behind the reasons', e.g. showing how the IMR affects birth rates, and then explaining why the IMR has fallen. There is not much evaluation here, but this is less important in an 'Examine' question. A separate concluding paragraph would be useful, but there is enough here for full marks.

(e) According to functionalists, the nuclear family of a married heterosexual couple and their children is functional for modern society because it provides geographical and social mobility, and functional for its members because it provides primary socialisation and stabilisation of adult personalities. For these reasons it is the norm. Likewise, Murdock sees it as universal because of its sheer practicality in performing vital functions.

However, the nuclear family now only accounts for a minority of families. Other types have increased – lone parents,, same-sex couples, cohabiting couples, reconstituted families, singletons. Unlike functionalists, the Rapoports see this growing diversity as good because it meets people's needs. They identify five types of diversity: organisational, cultural, class, life-cycle and generational.

Greater diversity has arisen for several reasons. Legal changes regarding divorce and homosexuality mean people are freer to create the relationships and families they want. Easier divorce (only having to prove 'irretrievable breakdown') means individuals (especially women, who account for 70% of petitions) can escape an unsatisfactory marriage. This often results in the creation of a matrifocal lone-parent family and a one-person household, and thus greater diversity. Similarly, civil partnerships may encourage same-sex couples.

Changing attitudes to personal relationships and sexuality are also important in creating diversity. Weeks argues that the state now has little say in intimate relationships and the norm is now one of tolerance of diversity and choice. Secularisation means the churches have lost influence so their opposition to things like abortion is ignored. There is now less stigma to being divorced, gay, cohabiting or having children outside marriage than 50 years ago. This means alternatives to the nuclear family can flourish.

Another factor is the change in women's position. Women are now better educated, more likely to be in work and more self-confident. The impact of feminism has encouraged women to demand equality and resist oppression. This has led many to seek alternatives to the nuclear family, including cohabitation and lone parenthood.

Postmodernists explain this diversity in terms of greater individualism, choice and gender equality. Beck argues that individualism has undermined the patriarchal family where everyone had fixed roles. Now we have the negotiated family, where individuals are free to leave if it doesn't meet their needs. This makes it more apt to break down, resulting in more diverse and fragmented family forms.

However, Chester argues that diversity has been overstated – most people still live in nuclear families, marry and don't divorce, most children are brought up by both parents etc. The only important change is a move from the conventional family, with male instrumental and female expressive roles, to the 'neo-conventional' family – like Young and Willmott's symmetrical family, where both spouses work.

Chester recognises that most people at any one time do not live in nuclear families, because of the life cycle – some young adults will not yet have married and had children, while many older adults will be 'empty-nesters' whose children have left home. Yet most people will create a nuclear family at some stage.

Chester notes that although cohabitation has increased, it is a temporary phase before marriage, while most divorcees re-marry. This suggests that marriage – a key feature of the nuclear family – remains the norm or ideal standard of behaviour for most people.

Part of the answer to the question depends on the definition of a nuclear family. The narrower the definition, the less it will be the 'norm'. For example, if children have to be the biological offspring of both parents, then stepfamilies won't count. Similarly, do the parents have to be married? A third of all children are born to cohabiting couples, which may be as stable as many marriages. Do parents have to be of the opposite sex? Same-sex couples can get a civil partnership and adopt. I would argue these are all nuclear families.

This raises issues about whether sociologists' definitions are better than those of the people they study. Many cohabiting couples (gay or straight) with children (own or adopted) see themselves as nuclear families. I agree with postmodernist views that if those concerned see themselves as a nuclear family, then they are one. However, I would conclude that if we wanted to say the nuclear family remains the norm, we have to accept that the definition must be widened because of the major changes in family patterns in recent decades.

(24/24)

> **Examiner's Comments**
> This answer shows a wide range of knowledge of relevant studies, theories, reasons and evidence. It is well focused on the issue of whether or not the nuclear family is still the norm. It gives the answer a theoretical context at the outset (functionalism) and then presents a range of counter-evidence on the growing diversity of family types, and analyses the possible reasons for this growth (legal and attitudinal changes, and changes in women's position). It puts this into the theoretical context of postmodernism, and then evaluates this using evidence and arguments from Chester. It questions the definition of the nuclear family and offers a reasoned and balanced conclusion.

Top Marks Answers for Unit 2

The answers below to the Practice Paper questions on page 85 all scored full marks.

Answer to Question 1

(a) This is when schools are allowed to compete with each other for pupils just as companies compete with each other for business. It involves giving parents choice so they become the customers of schools.

(b) Reasons are different parental expectations for girls and boys; subject channelling by teachers; peer group pressure; gendered careers and training.

> **Examiner's Comments**
> 1(a) The answer identifies and describes key features of an education market.
> 1(b) Four correct reasons. Giving a fourth one is a good strategy, in case one of your earlier ones is wrong.

(c) There are pro-school and anti-school subcultures. A pupil subculture is a set of shared values and behaviour patterns in relation to school. Pro-school subcultures reflect the mainstream values of the school.

Anti-school subcultures can take several forms but they all reject some or all school values. For example, Sewell found that a minority of black pupils formed a highly visible rebel subculture, rejecting school rules and acting in a 'macho' manner. Others were 'innovators', pro-education but anti-school, so they worked but didn't seek teacher approval. The majority however, conformed to school values.

Anti-school subcultures are a response to teacher labelling. Becker discovered how teachers' notion of an 'ideal pupil' leads them to expect different behaviour from pupils of different backgrounds. These expectations, as the Oak study showed, become real as teachers apply their expectations to their pupils. Teacher expectations can become part of the school system itself. Streaming reflects attitudes towards pupils of different social backgrounds and genders.

Unequal treatment produces a negative reaction from pupils labelled. Lacey found that boys – usually from working-class families – placed in lower streams, lost self-esteem. Gillborn and Youdell claim that teachers are quicker to discipline black boys and interpret their body language as being aggressive. The result is that unless the pupils conform, they create subcultures to help them deal with their situation.

All these explanations see anti-school subcultures as a reaction to teacher attitudes or school processes, but factors outside school also contribute. Sewell suggests that the absence of male role models at home has an effect. The decline in traditional 'male jobs' is another factor outside school that might lead to the creation of an anti-school subculture, as male pupils may feel there is little point in working. Media images of the 'gangsta rapper' also may lead some pupils into anti-school attitudes. However, what sociologists do not really know, is why different pupils form the different subcultures they do. $\frac{12}{12}$

> **Examiner's Comments**
> This answer considers mainly school factors but also mentions non-school causes as well – most answers would not cover the latter area. Several reasons are not simply stated but explained as well which leads to extra marks for analysis. Applying studies also gains application marks.

1d) Functionalists identify two main functions of education – maintaining value consensus and preparing young people for work. Although these are often the stated aims of education, Marxists disagree, stating that education legitimates and promotes class inequality. Feminists also do not accept that there is a value consensus, but argue instead that patriarchal attitudes dominate society.

Durkheim emphasised the importance of teaching society's shared history. This gives new members of society – children – a sense of shared identity based on the past. For example, in the USA, pupils swear an oath of allegiance to their country every day.

Parsons argues that education is a bridge between the individual's life in the family and their future life in wider society. The family's particularistic values (where the individual child is treated as special), have to give way to the universalistic values of wider society where everyone is, or should be, treated the same. Without this value consensus, society would not be able to continue, people would have different values, act differently towards each other and society would fall into anarchy.

Davis and Moore developed the functionalist argument that the education system is meritocratic. This enables those with the most talent and effort to fill the most important work roles in society. This creates the most efficient society, as the right people fill their roles based on their ability. Education is crucial here not just for supplying the training for these roles but for 'sorting and sifting' young people into the correct work. So those with limited academic ability are directed into manual, low skilled jobs.

However, functionalist views ignore the inequalities inside the education system. They present the relationship between education, society and the individual as a fair, smooth-running operation with good outcomes. Marxists argue that the system does not operate like this. In the first place, they claim that although there is a set of core values, these are not agreed but enforced from above. Althusser claims that education is an ideological state apparatus – a way of keeping control of the exploited working class by controlling how they think. There is no agreed set of values – education reproduces the values of the ruling class.

Similarly, Bowles and Gintis argue that education reproduces and legitimates inequality. The system does not operate meritocratically – this is a myth to convince people that their failure is their own fault rather than the system's. The amount and continuing nature of inequalities in educational achievement are proof that the system is inherently unfair and that people end up with the jobs they get because of their class and ethnic background, not their ability.

Marxists agree that education does prepare pupils for work but not how functionalists believe. Schools reward traits such as obedience and passivity. This prepares working-class pupils for the mindless manual work that awaits them, which in turn helps to support the capitalist system. Willis showed how 'the lads' formed an anti-school subculture that ironically prepared them for unskilled work. Furthermore, feminists argue that education's main function is to maintain patriarchal society. The 'male gaze', double standards in education and the lack of female head teachers in secondary schools all contribute to this process.

So although education might have the appearance of socialising young people into a value consensus, in reality this might be more a case of making the system work for particular social groups rather than for the whole population. (20/20)

> **Examiner's Comments**
> There is good coverage of functionalist views – Durkheim, Parsons, Davis and Moore. The material is kept tightly related to the question. The Marxist material is about the right length and detail and is also connected to the two functions. It's also applied evaluatively. In several places, the answer returns to the 'value consensus vs. ruling-class values' debate and to how education prepares pupils for work, but interpreted differently by functionalist and Marxist writers. The feminist material is an added bonus.

Answer to Question 2

Participant observation has the great strength of seeing what people do rather than hearing or reading what they say they do. This is a big advantage when studying pupils, especially younger pupils, as their language is less developed than adults'. Interpretivists see this as a huge strength, since PO increases the validity of the data created. However, it is debatable whether this is a genuine advantage when studying teacher attitudes towards male and female pupils.

As Item B suggests, teachers have a professional role to maintain. Part of that role is treating all pupils fairly and equally, regardless of their gender, ethnicity etc. Indeed, any teacher found to be acting in a clearly sexist manner could face disciplinary action. Therefore there is every reason for them to try to cover up any such behaviour in the school. Because they are unlikely to admit to treating pupils differently in an interview or questionnaire, then if the PO could be carried out covertly, it's far more likely that teachers would act naturally and not put up their defences.

Unfortunately, for a number of reasons connected to the nature of schools, it is unlikely that covert PO can be carried out. The classroom is a very limited space, so there is no opportunity for an observer to just 'hang about'. There are also very few social roles in a classroom – pupil, teacher and classroom assistant. Unless the researcher can covertly occupy one of these, their presence will put the teacher on their guard. Finally, the presence of young people in the classroom raises another problem for covert observation, which is that their vulnerability means that getting permission to study them is even more important.

However, what an observer might do is to sit in the staffroom and generally 'hang about' there, listening in on conversations. The staffroom is 'backstage' where teachers are more relaxed and off-guard, so the observer is more likely to see and hear what they really think about male and female pupils. In this case, the data generated will be more valid.

It may also be the case that with the head teacher's permission, it might be possible for the observer to present themselves as a teacher or supply teacher so they would be more likely to be accepted by other teachers. The head is a very powerful 'gatekeeper' in a school and their support is crucial to researchers.

The gender of the researcher is also likely to be an issue in this case. If the observation is overt and the observer female, some male teachers may assume that she is a feminist researcher with a particular agenda. These teachers may well act up or make extra efforts to hide their true attitudes as a result.

All of this illustrates the flexible nature of a 'go-with-the-flow' research method like PO. However, it also shows why positivists have little time for PO. It is totally unstructured in its approach and therefore cannot be replicated. The data is therefore not reliable. Nor is it likely to be representative as the samples are small and put together haphazardly.   (20/20)

> **Examiner's Comments**
> This is an excellent answer that focuses very clearly on the research opportunities and problems of using PO to study this particular issue. It takes a very interesting and effective approach to this type of question. Rather than listing strengths and weaknesses of PO and then trying to attach aspects of the particular research issue to this list, it identifies some of the research problems and opportunities of the issue and then links these to the strengths and limitations of PO. Even if an answer did this just a few times, it would really boost the mark.

Answer to Question 3

(a) This is when a study is repeated over time. The same sample is asked questions or observed periodically. The data is comparable.

(b) Firstly, there are too many variables in a real–life situation for the observer to control (and the researcher may not know what all the variables are in that situation). Secondly, field experiments are not suited to researching large-scale social behaviour patterns such as class and achievement.

(c) Two techniques are quota sampling and random sampling.

> **Examiner's Comments**
> 3(a) This answer identifies three characteristics of a longitudinal study – easily enough for the two marks.
> 3(b) Two suitable problems suggested.
> 3(c) Two relevant techniques identified. This is all that is needed – no explanation or description is required.

(d) Interviews take different forms, the main division being between structured and unstructured. Positivists favour structured interviews because they believe there is an objective social reality 'out there' that can be scientifically studied. To study something scientifically means that the researcher has to use methods that are reliable and representative. The result is data that is quantitative and that can be presented in the form of statistics. From these, researchers can see patterns and trends in behaviour.

This means using methods that are standardised. Structured interviews are standardised because they use the same set of questions for everyone. They also often use a limited range of responses from which respondents must choose their answer, which makes the creation of numerical data even easier. However, interpretivists see structured interviews as fundamentally flawed because they force interviewees to respond in ways decided by the researcher, not in ways they'd like to themselves.

Using a fixed set of questions and answers also means that the data from interviews is directly comparable. Structured interviews are easily replicable and therefore can be used to verify the results of other interviews. They also enable the researcher to compare responses over time in a longitudinal study. If the questions and answers were different in each interview, as in unstructured and group interviews, this could not be done.

Another big advantage is that structured interviews have a higher response rate than postal questionnaires. This is because it is more difficult for possible interviewees to refuse to be involved when asked personally, face-to-face. Together with the fact that structured interviews are much quicker to carry out than unstructured interviews, this means that a larger sample cam be studied. This increases the chances of the sample being representative – although it also depends on whether a stratified sample can be found. Positivists see this as a big advantage as it means the researcher can then make generalisations on the basis of the results from the sample. This forms part of the scientific technique favoured by positivists. Of course, interpretivists would argue that there is little point in getting representativeness if the data collected lacks meaning. Lack of validity makes the data irrelevant whether or not it is representative.

Structured interviews partially overcome a major weakness with unstructured interviews. In face-to-face interviews, the researcher's presence can affect the interviewee's responses. This reduces the validity of the data since the responses are not exactly what the interviewee would otherwise have given. In open-ended, free-flowing unstructured interviews, there is far more scope for responses to be influenced by the interviewer, no matter how skilled they are. When the interview is structured, a list of questions is simply asked and in some cases, researchers do this in a 'deadpan' manner, giving off body language that is as neutral as possible. This helps to maintain validity. However, interpretivists argue that the fixed lists of questions with no opportunity to investigate meanings in depth, means that the data from structured interviews lacks validity anyway.

Overall then, it is mainly positivists who see advantages in using structured interviews. Certainly they may be more suitable for gathering basic data and for investigating issues that are less sensitive. However, for issues such as domestic violence or racism, unstructured interviewing may be more appropriate.

20/20

> **Examiner's Comments**
> This answer makes good use of theory (positivism and interpretivism) and explains the link between structured interviews and positivism particularly well. There is accurate use of a range of relevant concepts. The answer retains a clear focus on the advantages of structured interviews and uses the weaknesses of the method in an appropriately evaluative way.

Your Notes